For
Jacob, George, Arthur
and the Folding Family

The Folding Lady

Tools & tricks to make the most of your space & find after value in your home

Sophie Liard

yellow
kite

First published in Great Britain in 2022 by Yellow Kite
An Imprint of Hodder & Stoughton
An Hachette UK company

Illustrations by Lydia Blagden © Hodder & Stoughton 2022

Text design by James Ward

Author photo on page 221 by Max Rose-Fyne © Hodder & Stoughton 2022

A CIP catalogue record for this title is available from the British Library

Hardback 978 1 529 38526 7
Ebook 978 1 529 38527 4

Typeset in Stratos by Production Type
Printed and bound in Great Britain by Clays Ltd, Elcograf S.p.A.

Hodder & Stoughton policy is to use papers that are natural, renewable and recyclable products and made from wood grown in sustainable forests. The logging and manufacturing processes are expected to conform to the environmental regulations of the country of origin.

Yellow Kite
Hodder & Stoughton Ltd
Carmelite House
50 Victoria Embankment
London EC4Y 0DZ

www.yellowkitebooks.co.uk

CONTENTS

INTRODUCTION

Here we are at the beginning of my first book. I'm so happy and grateful that you are reading this. I'm Sophie, aka The Folding Lady, and these beautiful pages have allowed me to bring together all my thoughts about, and passion for, folding and organisation.

For me, it's not just about the folding and sorting out though – I'm not a professional organiser, my experience is in retail and that's where the folding comes from. I'm a person who has come to recognise that my home is the most important space in my life – but I had to learn that. I'm Mum to two boys, and over the years, as my family has grown and I have grown up, I've had to work out and understand the changing needs and priorities in my home. I've put this learning together with my folding, and there are a whole host of ideas and skills I want to pass on to you so that you too can improve your relationship with your space, and make the most of the home you have. It really can be life-changing!

YOUR SPACE IS A TOOL

Being 'organised' goes so much deeper than it appears to on the surface. Social media shows us all these glorious images and stories of beautifully organised homes, and it can often feel like such things are out of our reach. It certainly does to me. The truth is that those pictures are of someone else's home and dream and life. What is missing is any connection to our own needs and wants, and the place where we live.

Your home can truly support you to live the life you want to lead if you set it up in a way that's authentic to you and the other people who live there. Once you recognise your home as a haven to make the everyday less chaotic, an easier life – a less stressed life and a life that is unique to you, and no one else – will start to come into view. That's when the magic really starts to happen.

I want to help you to recognise when your space is the catalyst to bad vibes, and show you how to make it a healing place. We're going to uncover how your home can provide more of what you truly need, encourage you to do more of the things you love, to be more creative, and to be more honest about who you really are. And everything in-between. And you can achieve all this through nothing fancy – no excessive expense or time – but merely by setting up your home in a way that reflects your needs and desires.

CREATING 'AFTER VALUE'

By the end of this book you will understand how making decisions based on After Value – and this alone – has been life-changing for many of my followers. If you don't understand this phrase 'After Value', there's a whole section on it later but, in short, After Value is the positive feeling, reason for or result of doing/buying something that is motivated by our own wants and needs, our goals and priorities. Not what we see others doing and having, not what social media and advertising tell us will improve our lives forever.

And we get to find the After Value in our homes by making a RESET of our space – organising, reworking, rearranging or tweaking how we use our homes for maximum After Value.

> "
> **We're going to get you organising your home with meaning and emotion, rather than just copying something you saw and liked online.**
> "

After Value will become your new currency for living a life that is so much more than folding your socks and jeans in a pretty impressive way. It goes beyond aesthetic pleasure and tidy shelves, it is about *YOU* and your time, your goals and your purpose for getting up in the morning, and the decisions you make every day. It's about working out what is important for you, what gives you comfort, and perhaps what gives you back that piece of yourself that you lost somewhere along the way. We're going to get you organising your home with meaning and emotion, rather than just copying something you saw and liked online.

WHAT I WANT THIS BOOK TO DO FOR YOU

If you are someone who doesn't like their home, who's not happy with how their space works or what it says, someone who constantly finds it difficult to manage their belongings and is never on top of it all, then together we are going to change that mindset and have you raring to go on your home RESET for maximum After Value and ready to fall back in love with your space.

To help with this, *Part 1: Create Your Space* is my manifesto about how you can change your personal space to change your life – maximising its functionality while creating something that helps you to understand more about what you really want from life. It's going to be good – with small tweaks or big changes, you can make your space work for you and your goals.

Part 2: The Folding Guide is a guide to all of my most transformative folds, accompanied by lots of my favourite organising hacks and tips. These are the folds that my followers have told me have made their spaces much easier to manage, given them so much more room, and also made doing the never-ending tasks like the laundry an activity they look forward to and power through in their daily routines.

ORGANISE ACCORDING TO VALUE

We should all love our home, whether it's the one we dreamed of or not. It's important to be able to feel grateful for what we have in the present, and the people within it. If you're always striving for something and somewhere else, then, believe me, you will be striving forever. Make peace with what you have at the moment. We are going to work on this together, and together we will make it a truly rewarding experience.

Using After Value as your new currency to make decisions around your home will make it a happier and more enjoyable space for everyone. Start organising for your actual lifestyle rather than what you want your lifestyle to be. Learn to love your home as it is and recognise when it's not too small, you just have too much stuff; or when it's not the wrong

> **"**
>
> **Using After Value as your new currency to make decisions around your home will make it a happier and more enjoyable space for everyone.**
>
> **"**

shape, you just have to adapt to the space or needs of your current lifestyle.

And just remember, not every single bit of the book may resonate right now. But I guarantee some of it will. This is not a rule book; no one makes up the rules for your home except you. Use this book as inspiration, understanding that the way your home is set up should reflect your present priorities and no one else's. This means you may have to tweak some of the things I show you but the basics are there.

Some elements will work perfectly but with others you may need to use your common sense and adapt them to suit your home or lifestyle. Life is an ever-changing journey and there may be a time when, say, you have a baby and you pick the book back up to learn the baby folds – just one example. So keep the book safe because you may want to dip back in some time in the future. As my cousin, Aelish, says 'take what resonates in the present and leave the rest for now', which is a great way of thinking.

***

I can't wait for you to read this book. I feel like it's going to be a game-changer for us all! Just remember, each one of us is unique... no two households are the same.

PART

CREATE YOUR SPACE

THE BEGINNING

It's about time I told you a little about me and where I've come from – my back story if you will. I'm going to explain how I became a master clothes folder, and how that passion and skill led me to where I am, sat in my kitchen, writing this book. And how I went viral on TikTok in lockdown, resulting in the platform I have now where we, the #foldingfam, meet and share our love for all things home life.

HOW DID THE BOOK HAPPEN?

You've probably heard of The Folding Lady online (@thefoldinglady), teaching you how to fold, organise and gift wrap. I give some authentic snippets of my home life there but my account is not about me so much as the folding, so I should introduce myself properly...

My name is Sophie and I'm 36 years old. I grew up in Crumpsall, in Greater Manchester, England, with my mum, dad and older sister. My dad was a bus driver and my mum a nurse. When I was about 10, my mum got a job in Surrey so we all moved in with my gran who lived there. After secondary school [translation: high school – there's a handy UK to US terms glossary on page 233 to solve any language questions], I went on to college but it wasn't right for me and so I left after a term.

In the meantime, I had started working at the weekends in a department store and I took on a full-time job there. My first son, George, was born when I was 21 and I decided to give studying another go so I began a degree in Early Childhood Studies and graduated with a First Class Honours when I was 25. I fully intended to continue on to achieve my Qualified Teacher status but personal circumstances saw me working back at the department store again, where I had continued working part-time throughout my degree.

At this time I lived in what many of you will know as The Flat near Guildford, just outside London, with George. A few years later, I met my husband, Jacob, and he also moved in to the flat with George and me. We got married in November 2016 and along came Arthur in December 2018 to complete our family. Last year we finally moved out of The Flat to the house you see us in today.

As I've got older I've learnt how to live more in the present. I've spent a lot of time on myself over the last few years, discovering how to take real responsibility for my own happiness and health. Now I focus on the good in my life, and the things that make me happy. I try and steer clear of the bad but when that's not possible I am a lot better at tolerating it.

I am happy, positive, practical and like to have a good laugh. I'm a Capricorn so I am also hot-headed, argumentative and easily irritated. I love to read and to educate myself, I am fascinated by watching my kids grow up – human behaviours in general intrigue me. I love food, Prosecco and a good old Jägerbomb on a night out with my girlfriends!

My folding journey, and the start of my understanding about After Value and taking responsibility for my own choices, truly began at the department store. . .

MY FIRST FOLD

'Where did you learn to fold?' is one of the most common questions I get asked, and I remember my first folding experience as if it was yesterday.

I was 16 and it was my first day at the department store. I immediately felt at home. I walked through security, signed in with my name and time of entry, strolled through the locker room, up the stairs and through the door that led to the shop floor.

As I walked down the aisle towards the back of the shop floor, I had no idea where I needed to be but I was drawn to the wall of denim. Piles and piles of Diesel jeans were beautifully folded on columns of shelves, with a big table in front where there were more piles of jeans. Each pile was of a particular jean style and you could see they were in perfect size order from largest at the bottom to smallest at the top. Then, above the shelves, there was a pair of jeans attached to the wall to show it off in all its glory to customers. It was organised, made the most of the space and was aesthetically pleasing.

I was fascinated by the way the jeans were folded but I couldn't figure out how it was done at first glance. There were the same number of pairs of jeans in each pile, and it made me happy just looking at them; it soothed me and filled me with instant calm. There were a few pairs of jeans out of place to one side and my brain didn't like this so I couldn't help myself. I picked up a pair and started to fold.

'That is not how you fold my jeans!' came a sharp voice from behind me. 'This is my section but, as you are here, I'll show you how to do it properly.'

And that was the moment I learnt my first fold. And it was not just any fold. I would say the Diesel jeans fold is one of the most iconic I came across during my 15 years in retail. Many attempted it and few passed the test. I did, of course, but not on that first day – much more practice was needed but I had caught the folding bug already. By the end of my first day, I was hooked.

I was initially hired as a Christmas temp to work on Saturdays, but after my short stint at college didn't work out, Mum made me ask my manager for more hours. Mum gave me two options – I could go back to college and she and Dad would support me by giving me lunch money and train fare, or I could get a full-time job and pay them rent. I come from a family of workers so me staying at home doing nothing just wasn't going to happen. At 16 I really had no idea what I wanted to do so neither of these options felt exciting to choose from but I enjoyed my Saturday job the most so full-time at the store it was!

MERCHANDISING

Soon I was working in womenswear as a sales assistant in the French Connection department. They had a great mixture of hanging rails and shelves filled with knits, jeans and tops so I quickly learnt how to fold from my colleagues. I was taught how to use folding paper to make the jumpers look neat and uniform in size, and how to fold clothes into a pile by size. I also had to learn how to 'merchandise' rails with appealing outfit options and according to prescribed colour stories from the brand, and how to move around the fixtures and fittings to make the department look fresh and new to the customers on a regular basis.

Merchandising was one of those jobs that you were either good at or not. It involved a vision and knowledge for colours, current and seasonal trends, the needs of the customers and so many other elements. It wasn't just about moving the clothes around; it was about making the most of the space, thinking up new ways to display clothes and making sure branding was in place. Some brands would send merchandising guidelines but they didn't always suit the space. A good merchandiser would be able to take the guidance and adjust it to their space and stock. The main goal was to keep your department looking new and fresh for customers and to showcase your best-selling products with the aim of making sales.

The possibilities were endless and I enjoyed this side of the job so much. I longed to oversee the creative aspect of the role rather than just taking direction from someone else. I liked my colleagues' ideas but I was bursting with thoughts about ways to make the products look amazing but also organise the department to make the customers' shopping experience easier and more pleasant. There was nothing better for me than the end-of-the-day 'folding and hanger-spacing time' alone with my creative thoughts.

IN CHARGE

My time finally came when I was put in charge of the DKNY concession. I'd begged my manager for this department and eventually got it. I felt like I'd truly landed. It was a good size, had its own till point and three fitting rooms. I was 17 and, in my eyes, I was the manager of my own shop. I bought myself a notepad, pen and calculator. The brand paid half my wages so I told everyone very proudly that I worked for DKNY. I received a free uniform every six months and they were the most expensive clothes I owned. I felt like I was in *Sex and the City* working for such a luxurious brand. I would buy *Vogue* magazine every month to keep up-to-date with high-end fashion. I can't tell you how much I loved this job and this brand. Over the next two years I lived and breathed this department, never caring what time I left work, and when I eventually did, not a fold or a hanger would be out of place.

Over the next 15 years in the department store I folded and wrapped hundreds of different brands, from 7 For All Mankind to the iconic Victoria Beckham crown pocket jeans, from Ralph Lauren polos to Armani T-shirts. I had folds that allowed me to get more clothes on the fixture because it was Christmas, folds that would make the clothing look so special it had to be purchased, folds that piled the clothes high ready for sale shoppers, folds to show brand logos, folds that were fun, folds that were luxury... the list went on. I worked my way up to Floor Manager and worked across all of the departments: Mens, Ladies and Fashion Accessories. I ended my time at the store with a year running the Cosmetics department so my organising skills and product knowledge covered a broad range of products.

THE JOY OF GIFT WRAPPING

I love gift wrapping. No one deserves more respect for wrapping than a retailer because we get no training (except what we teach each other), hardly any resources and we have to learn to fold and wrap a purchase with the customer watching and another customer waiting.

The pressure is intense but we aim to be quick and efficient. The appreciation from customers for even a simple wrap in a single piece of tissue is just lovely. I think a lot of retailers really underestimate that last part of the customer journey when they've paid for their item and the exchange of ownership is about to happen. Those of us who understand this moment fully would fold the item nicely, wrapping it beautifully in tissue so it doesn't unravel in the bag. I liked to hand it over with a parting congratulatory comment like, 'Great purchase, it's a beautiful top. Enjoy!' And I would really mean it because so many of the items are high-end and way out of my own price range. We were genuinely so in love with a lot of the products. Sometimes we were actually sad to see them go!

My favourite wrap is the one we used every day. Gift or no gift, if we had tissue paper available on our till point we would use the simple but clever 'tissue paper, no tape' wrap. I remember watching Mel in the Whistles department doing this wrap so quickly and seamlessly for all their customers and I made her show me how to do it. It was a game-changer for my customer service – the joy people got from watching me wrap their clothes was amazing. It was such a great end to their experience in the store, they were always so grateful. This is why I love gift wrapping so much; it brings such After Value and happiness to both the giver and the recipient.

MILESTONES

A lot of my life milestones were at the department store... I turned 18 and 21 while I was there, had my first work night out, my first pay cheque, first promotion, finished my degree and had my first baby! During my pregnancy with George, I worked in the denim department and I spent those months folding jeans – 7 For All Mankind, Hudson, Paige Jeans and Levi's – sometimes standing, sometimes sat on a little stool I was given. It was pure bliss! I also made some friends for life – four of whom are godmothers to George and Arthur, and many more who I regularly see and speak to.

I have such great memories from the years I worked in the store, and professionally I learnt a lot, so I will forever be grateful for the experience. The 'visions and values' – that's what the company called them – I learnt over the years are ones I took home with me, along with the folding and display methods. Values such as respect for others, working as a team, calling the customers 'sir' and 'madam', attention to detail, learning to train and develop people – I have so many transferable skills that I have carried with me into my other work and home life.

FROM STORE
TO HOME

"

The store was a never-ending cycle of new season, mid-season, promos, sales, Easter, summer and Christmas, and working in a job like this helped me make peace with the reality that keeping a home tidy, clean and organised is an ongoing daily process, where the work is never over.

"

Well, it's safe to say my wardrobe at home was always in order. Ha!

My deeper thinking around the effects of folding and organisation didn't evolve until later, but the aesthetically pleasing displays were there from day one. My wardrobe was organised, drawers were tidy and I had a few nice displays. I didn't have a lot of stuff or fancy décor in my room or home as a retail salary didn't allow for that, but it was always clean and tidy and, most of all, there was an order to it. Different spaces were useful and had a purpose, because in the store I was used to being given a space and a range of products to curate a practical, beautiful display. We had to be a creative bunch when it came to displays because we wouldn't know what was coming in on a delivery and it all had to fit in the space available. Special times, such as sales and Christmas, saw us having to fit an incredible amount of stock in the departments and we did this like pros, while making sure everything looked beautiful and, most importantly, highly shoppable.

The store was a never-ending cycle of new season, mid-season, promos, sales, Easter, summer and Christmas, and working in a job like this helped me make peace with the reality that keeping a home tidy, clean and organised is an ongoing daily process, where the work is never over. Regular upkeep and commitment are necessary, but knowing that makes the day-to-day duties much more enjoyable work. This mindset is very relieving once you sign up for it.

SATISFACTION

At home I am driven by my excitement for each 'reset' of space – whether it is something major like redecorating or repurposing a space or merely updating some tired cushions. Just like in the store, rearranging my belongings (like the products) and resetting the space created After Value (the sales) and happiness for my family (just as for the customers).

What did translate to my home straight away was the ability to enjoy the task of folding and organising in itself. As with resetting a display, the satisfaction involved in pulling together objects into a practical and appealing arrangement is wonderful. What was also important was the ability to not be upset when things got messy or disorganised. After 15

> **"**
> **I don't see any of the folding as making something that is so perfect it shouldn't be touched. It has a purpose, and therefore must be used, looked at or enjoyed.**
> **"**

years of working in a shop, if I got upset with mess, I would be upset *a lot*. We didn't in the store because the mess meant good things there; it meant people were shopping and trying on clothes and, most importantly, that our displays were attracting people. I don't see any of the folding as making something that is so perfect it shouldn't be touched. It has a purpose, and therefore must be used, looked at or enjoyed. If I hadn't folded the jeans in size order and by style so beautifully, then the customers would not have been able to shop with such ease or success. Customers would have been left dissatisfied at failing to find their size or what they were looking for. And this really does apply to the home also. I don't find folding a labouring task, when an action has meaning and purpose it becomes enjoyable.

Then, when I was pregnant with Arthur and I realised I needed to fit two adults, a near-teenager and a baby into a two-bed flat happily, only then did I discover the real After Value of folding and organising in the home.

LIFE IN THE FLAT

If you've followed me on social media from the beginning, you may remember The Flat, where we lived for 15 years. It was a lovely-sized two-bed maisonette. It had two double bedrooms and an open-plan kitchen and living-room area which made it feel light and spacious. We lived on the first floor and the window in the living room had the most amazing view of the treetops outside that made it feel like you were living in the middle of nowhere. I positioned the sofa specifically to face that window and had many moments of calm in the storms of life looking out at the view. A lot of you will remember that view, hey?

When George's little friends came round, they would say we lived in a 'treehouse', which was a lovely turnaround from their initial shock that we only had one floor to our accommodation. 'Where is your downstairs?' was a common question. But they all loved our treehouse as much as we did.

The Flat was more than enough for the three of us but when we got pregnant with Arthur it became clear that it was too much of a squeeze for four. We wanted a garden and for the boys to have their own rooms, especially as George would soon be a teenager. I knew we needed to move.

A SENSIBLE DECISION

We had discussed moving before my maternity leave, but we realised money would be a struggle if we did and we just didn't want the stress of that. In the past I would have chosen to struggle with money and have the bigger home but logic told me that more After Value would come from waiting, being patient and having better finances while I was off work. A bigger house would not bring us happiness; it would lead to financial stress. We made a plan to stay and adapt the flat for our immediate needs, and then look into moving again in about three years' time. At that point, Arthur would be two and George would be 13.

A HOME FOR A COT

As part of the necessary 'reset', I reassessed the situation at home. My professional skills in making spaces into beautiful and practical areas came to the fore – it was time to properly use that skill in our home.

We started with our bedroom. There was a little nook that, when measured, proved to be a perfect fit for a baby cot. This currently housed my make-up desk, so I moved that nearer to the door. This was the most annoying position for it, but as a make-up and skincare addict it was my pride and joy and had to stay. It was important to me.

However, I realised I had eight drawers full of skincare and make-up, which at the time seemed necessary but now seems ridiculous. Over time, I purged it down to three drawers. After the first purge and RESET, I realised I didn't miss anything so, on reflection, I had wasted a lot of space. In the real world there's only so much make-up and skincare you can use at one time. It has taken me a long time to calm this addiction (the word hoarding is more appropriate) but I now have my hero products and will not allow myself to replace a product unless I have completely run out of it. I get so much more After Value from this new system. When I finish a pot of something the thrill of buying a new one means so much more. When I hand over my money now it has so much more intention and purpose. Also, I actually have the money to spend because I am not in debt from being a shopaholic. Anyway, I digress!

We looked at the floor plan of George's room and realised that we could move his desk into the outhouse [translation: not an outdoor toilet! This was a brick building just outside our front door]. Then we would free up a space for a cot so eventually the boys could share a bedroom. George was excited about sharing with his brother so this felt good.

> **"**
> **When I hand over my money now it has so much more intention and purpose.**
> **"**

George also had a wardrobe which took up a lot of space and was so tall that it made the room feel small. When I really thought about it, a lot of his clothes didn't need to be hung – after all, I was a clothing storage expert!

We sold the wardrobe and bought two sets of drawers from IKEA (the ones that feature on my TikTok at the very beginning), one of which we still have in his room. We hung his school uniform in our wardrobe and folded all his and Arthur's clothes into these drawers. At this moment I was folding alone; little did I know that a year later I'd be folding for millions!

ORGANISING AND PURGING

The folding worked perfectly and became a bit of a routine and obsession for me. I started to look forward to putting the washing away. We didn't have a dryer in the flat so I had a great routine with times for the washing machine to be on, then I moved the laundry to dry on two racks in the hallway (these drying racks never really came down) and then I would fold and put away the clothes straight from the rack. I completely stopped using my washing basket. It reignited my passion for merchandising and folding, and I would spend time making it all look nice.

> **" This wasn't about the cost but the space it would take up. Space was a much more valuable currency at this point to us than the pound. "**

I had perfected quick and easy folds for everyone's clothes by that time. And, as planned, we created the space we needed to be comfortable for the next three years. We purged the items that didn't give us any After Value and organised every drawer, cupboard and hanging space. We agreed to be more mindful when buying physical things that would be kept in the home – working out what had true purpose. This wasn't about the cost but the space it would take up. Space was a much more valuable currency at this point to us than the pound. It was the space I was creating that was the priority and giving us all true After Value at this point.

As I used more and more folds from store life, I found myself adapting or devising new folds that were more practical for us. For example, to avoid spending a few seconds buttoning up baby grows, I started to fold them on their backs and in half. This not only made putting the clothes away quicker but made changing Arthur a few seconds quicker as well. By folding socks I soon realised I was finding fewer and fewer odd socks, saving money on buying more.

MY KNICKER DRAWER!

One day I was going through my usual morning ritual of spending 15 minutes looking everywhere for a pair of my favourite black cotton 'Bridget Jones' knickers. This was not time well spent and was stressing me out before the school run and work. It was time to organise my underwear drawer!

When I had finished, I couldn't believe how many pairs of knickers were in there! Some that were brand new and not even worn had got lost under the mountain of underwear I had. I never thought I'd go as far as folding my underwear but I have folded and lined up my knickers ever since and never spend time looking for them now.

> **"**
>
> **It got to the point where everything had a place and everything that could be folded was folded.**
>
> **"**

The other thing about being able to see all your clothes in a row is that it makes you realise which clothes you really don't wear. This is a great reminder of the random impulse purchases or buys you often don't really need.

It wasn't long before I was using drawer inserts and drawer dividers. These kept everything in place, saving me more time and making the clothes look even more aesthetically pleasing in my drawers. It was so satisfying. It got to the point where everything had a place and everything that could be folded was folded. I was the official folder in my house. I always get asked if the boys do any folding, and the answer is 'no'. I enjoy it too much to let that job go.

PRIORITY: A FUNCTIONING HOME

Apart from reigniting my passion for organising, folding, merchandising and making things look nice, I realised how much fun the sorting process was. And how freeing it was to live a life where a functioning home was the main priority, and not how many pairs of trainers I had. When the space worked for me and my family, it was truly transformative. Not just for my mind – but also for my bank balance. I felt in control of everything and the centre of that wasn't money but my home and curating a space that felt calm, meaningful and had real purpose for how we lived and what was important to us.

This feeling has grown even more since moving to our house. I never thought I'd say that I get a bigger kick out of focusing on small, actionable tasks like preparing a roast, setting a table and organising a drawer than spending money in the shops or watching reality TV. And don't get me wrong, I absolutely love shopping and reality TV, but it's much more enjoyable when you're shopping for needs and true wants rather than just being caught up in the moment.

So how did all this folding get online?

TIKTOK

Fast forward to the Covid-19 pandemic in March 2020 and the first UK lockdown, where non-essential shops closed including most retailers, and I found myself on furlough. One day I was voice noting my friend Rhiannon and we both mentioned this social media app that had blown up in lockdown: TikTok. I had downloaded the app a year earlier but was informed by my teenage niece that it wasn't for me, so ended up never using it then. Rhiannon and I both wanted to start posting and thought we'd challenge ourselves. We decided to each post something really boring/random and see whose clip did the best. Rhiannon posted herself cleaning her carpet with a handheld pet hair duster. Her TikTok post did amazingly well, eventually reaching one million views. My first TikTok was a hack about how to get wax out of your wax melt, which didn't do as well.

> **"**
> **I felt in control of everything and the centre of that wasn't money but my home and curating a space that felt calm, meaningful and had real purpose for how we lived and what was important to us.**
> **"**

Then one day I was folding the boys' clothes and decided to film it. I showed a drawer of messy clothes and then the same drawer tidy, with all the clothes folded into my IKEA SKUBBs. It got a couple of thousand views plus some questions about the SKUBBs, which I was excited to reply to. I followed up with another couple of videos of me organising George's clothes and Arthur's baby grows that performed about the same. Next, I decided to show some folding so I propped up my phone on George's piggy bank (which took me longer than filming the video itself!) and filmed myself folding his T-shirts. This video got 400k views very quickly. I enjoyed the filming and, as I was already folding often, every time I put some clothes away or organised something I recorded it on my phone and posted.

At first, most of my videos were doing okay, then a leggings folding video got to 100k views, which was wild. And the folding George's football kit video was very popular. I started getting requests from people in the comments, and as TikTok has a function that allows you to respond with a video this became the go-to on my account. People requested folds and I would respond. Even if it was an odd question, there was always a purpose because a follower had requested it.

SOCKS

One day someone asked me to fold socks. I chose a pair of Jacob's Puma socks that were brand new and looked lovely and crisp and white on camera and 'ranger-rolled' them on the bed. It was a simple nine-second video, with no edits involved and just music added. I posted as normal not thinking anything of it. I remember logging on to TikTok the next day and seeing my notifications had reached a peak of '99+' and wondered what had happened. My first viral TikTok was in full motion. It's a bit crazy when you get a viral TikTok because it can all blow up very quickly. I went from 20k followers to 120k in the space of a few days and, wow, did I then have a lot of requests to fulfil.

It was a turning point for me when I had to say to myself: 1) you can no longer aim to fulfil all the requests because you would have to fold all day every day; and 2) this could be something really good so let's make a decision to take it seriously and see where it goes. The sock video is currently on 4.4 million views and I will forever remember it as a big moment for me.

After making the decision to take things a little more seriously, it was clear I had to work on the filming. So Jacob bought me a £10 phone holder (which I still use today), and I set up to film in the bedroom at the end of our bed on a grey blanket. It was such a simple set-up, which I thought was amazing. Looking back, I laugh at how shabby it was!

I would mostly go to work or have the kids in the day and then film at night. Sometimes I'd film in the daytime if I had a quiet moment. When the dark nights came, Jacob found me some professional lights so I could continue my filming pattern. Work, kids, fold, eat, sleep, repeat.

At this point, my account was still in my real name Sophie Liard. I was chatting about everything with my mum and my sister, Kelly, one evening and they were joking about me being The Folding Lady of TikTok. I thought that sounded silly and that they were making fun of me, but they were being serious. 'Did you not see that's what people call you in the comments?' they asked. We discussed me changing my name and it was the game-changer to making me a serious brand, and also to showing myself that this seemingly niche passion of mine could become something big.

THE FOLDING LADY IS BORN

As time went on, my channels continued to grow and I decided I needed someone to help me with branding. I put a story out on my Instagram one day asking for recommendations for someone who could design me a logo. I had hundreds of offers to design one for free but I said from the beginning that this was business and I wanted the full package and to pay full price. This was my branding and it was important to me; I had to be able to say if I didn't like it and to ask for changes. I wouldn't have felt like I could do that if I got something for free.

What stood out for me was an email I received from a guy called James. James' fiancée (now wife), Rosie, is one of my followers and she had told James about my story. He sent me an email with his portfolio attached and this just stood out to me and also felt right. Over the next month we worked together on what is the logo you see on all my platforms today. James continues to work on all my branding and is also the creative behind this book design and the cover. There's a handful of people who have been crucial to my journey from the beginning and James is one of them. So when I got the opportunity to write this book he was first on my list to draw into the process. Surround yourself with good people and bring them with you – this is something I always remind myself to do.

By this point, the question was being asked. . . when is the right time to quit my job and take The Folding Lady full-time. I had made a little cash, which I was saving to back me up when the time came, but I didn't know if it was sustainable to take the permanent jump. I'd lived a life working under a contract, with the security of a guaranteed pay cheque at the

"

Surround yourself
with good people
and bring them
with you – this is
something I always
remind myself to do.

"

end of every month. It seemed so out of control to let go of this security blanket. But could it bring better things? More After Value? I saved about six months' worth of pay cheques and decided the time was right. The feeling when I handed in my notice was incredible! It was time to really focus.

I had now taken an immense dive into the unknown realms of online content creation and brand building and it was pretty scary. One day a follower called Sarah reached out to me. She runs an extremely successful account called @gocleanco – now you know who I mean! She offered a phone call to discuss the world of social media as she herself had gone viral in lockdown. She explained her journey and how a major content creator had reached out to her when she had no clue and she wanted to do the same for me.

It's these moments where you just love to learn from others and I am full of gratitude for those individuals putting in their time and effort to advance my career. It also reminds me that you don't need to know it all because the people you surround yourself with are there to help. After all, at this point, I was basically in a brand new job with no induction training. I needed people like James and Sarah around me.

WHAT THIS BOOK CAN DO FOR YOU

One thing I would say about going viral on social media is that it isn't as easy as it looks. I genuinely treated it as a second job when I was still at work. A lot of people say 'you got lucky', but I do not believe in luck. Think about the person who won the lottery. They didn't win it through luck, they won it because they bought the ticket. It doesn't matter how small the action was compared to the prize, they still put themselves out there.

I got to where I am on my platforms because I put out the content. I showed up day after day, filming and fulfilling requests from my followers. I would analyse my insights to make sure I was aware of my trends and what my followers were enjoying and what was growing my platform. I put time aside to read the comments, to interact with people spending their time on my account and return some gratitude, and to understand what they wanted to see from me. I set up an Instagram and started to navigate my way round that platform, which is totally different to TikTok with a whole different set of followers. I was fully committed.

And although it was hard work, it was enjoyable. A regular follower of mine messaged me the other day and asked, 'When did you realise you were big news?' and when I think about it, I really don't think I've had that moment yet. From this side of the phone, I am still the same me, with the same lifestyle, eating the same food, getting annoyed at the same things, etc. I think if this had happened to me 10 years ago, I may have thought differently as celebrities and people with public profiles seemed like a different species. But as you grow in life you realise everyone is the same, they just have their own unique values and that it doesn't matter if you're famous on Instagram, or a retailer or a doctor. . . Ultimately, we're all human.

> **"**
> **The life I choose to lead isn't comparable to anyone else's, because it's mine.**
> **"**

I see other humans as unique, rather than different to me. The life I choose to lead isn't comparable to anyone else's, because it's mine.

"

Success is defined
by the After Value
you recognise
and create for
your authentic self.

"

That way, we are all worthy in the same way. Success is defined by your happiness, the After Value you recognise and create for your authentic self. Take me writing this book, for example; I love books and it's beyond amazing that I have been gifted the opportunity to write my own. The After Value for me is, well, through the roof on this one. BUT that is not comparable to someone else who wouldn't be fussed about writing a book; they wouldn't understand how I feel.

The big news is all the successes I see and the After Value coming out of this platform I have – and I see that in the photos I receive every day of folded clothes in your homes, your children folding, spaces that have been purged and RESET, homes that reflect you and not what you see online, and your eased anxiety from watching my videos. So it's not about me alone; it's about you, your homes, the people in them, the good vibes we are creating and the community we have. The Folding Lady would be nothing without everyone else. If anyone is big news it's us, as a collective, as the #foldingfam.

WHAT IS
AFTER VALUE?

I used to live a life where I would make decisions based on every outside factor except what made me happy. I'd buy things that social media told me would make my kitchen smarter. I'd buy things that were on sale or that everyone else was buying. I'd buy the things I thought I should buy. And then I couldn't understand why they didn't change my life, improve my self-esteem or make my day better... It was when I started recognising the After Value in my purchases and the decisions I was making, and I used it as the reasoning behind my choices, that my life changed for the better.

After Value is a positive feeling, a confirmation, a reason, a value for doing something – whether it's spending time with someone or buying a product. It's a currency for living that goes beyond organising and folding, and is more than the aesthetics of your living space. It doesn't involve anyone else but you – your time, your goals and your choices. Every day. It's not based on anyone else's opinions or influence, but purely on your own wants, needs and desires – what is important to you, what gives you comfort and what helps you to reclaim those parts of yourself that have got lost along the way in life. You'll never feel guilt when you use After Value as a currency because it's authentic. It's made by your asking, 'Why am I buying this?' Or a reflection on, 'Was this good for me, and why?'

> **"**
> **After Value is a positive feeling, a confirmation, a reason, a value for doing something – whether it's spending time with someone or buying a product.**
> **"**

The answers to these types of questions, when answered openly and honestly, is part of the process of assessing your inner values. Sometimes this is an uncomfortable one because it goes against 'the norm' and can tell you what you don't want to hear (like when I needed to get rid of my 8 drawers of make-up) but, honestly, it's the absolute right answer (and I would never go back to 8 drawers of make-up again). I know something is giving me After Value because it's helping me live the life I want to lead – a better, much happier, authentic life. What also shows up for a lot of people is that the actions that give them the most After Value are actions that they previously told themselves they didn't have time for, so it can really help you devise a new set of priorities for yourself.

It's important to explain how I used to think, to show you how I came to use After Value to make changes. If you'd asked me 10 years ago how I assessed what was worthy of being in my life, what was worthy of having money spent on it and what my views were on what made me happy, my answers would have been very different to what they are now. These are the honest truths of where I used to be:

'THE CHEAPER THE BETTER'

I was tight with money. I mean I wasn't rich so this was valid at times, but I would actively avoid spending money. Or so I thought. I was in this mindset of 'I can't afford anything', yet if I added up the monetary value of the stuff I bought in Primark, thinking I was staying cheap, I had plenty of spare money that could have been better spent on something that gave me After Value. I had a 'quantity-over-quality' mentality, something we all so often fall victim to. For the 50+ Primark items I bought over the course of a couple of years, I could have saved up and bought a quality designer piece that would have lasted me a lifetime and I'd still have it now.

I made purchases based on how cheap they were, desperate for an instant shopping buzz, but also wanting a bargain. What that bargain ended up being was more stuff I didn't need and less space in my home though. And very quickly the buzz of buying this great purchase was gone. To make it worse, when it came to assessing my spending each month, I could see that I was wiping out all of my pay cheque. Seeing how wasteful I was and reflecting on it was such a depressing exercise and all I could think about was how I could have bought that new vacuum cleaner I needed and said I couldn't afford, or taken the kids on that day out I said was too expensive. I could have even booked a holiday with a few months of these habits. It was a toxic cycle, whereby with the stuff I was buying I was expecting to find happiness but always finding sadness.

PEOPLE PLEASING

I actually still struggle with this one, but I have an awareness of it so have managed to improve a lot. Years ago I would people please so much more. I would wear what someone suggested just so I didn't have to disagree with their opinion, I would go for lunches even though I didn't really want to and needed the money for other things, and I ate certain foods because they were in magazines and I thought it would impress people if I told them; you get the idea. But I also would make choices for myself with other people in mind even if they didn't know!

All of this added up to an inauthentic way of living and I really had no idea who I truly was. What did I like? Who did I like? What kind of mum did I want to be? And so on. I was too busy worrying about how pleased other people would be by my actions that I forgot to check in with what I really wanted to do.

ALWAYS WANTING WHAT SOMEONE ELSE HAS

I wanted what 'she' had. I wanted what I couldn't afford. I wanted everything that I really couldn't have and that didn't make sense for my financial position or even my lifestyle. And I just wanted it because I wanted to copy all those people online and in advertisements that were selling this dream life. I would jump on every trend possible just to feel part of it, to feel a connection to the way advertising made me feel I should and could be, and that desired connection only ever came about 10% of the time.

> **I would jump on every trend possible just to feel part of it, to feel a connection to the way advertising made me feel I should and could be, and that connection only ever came about 10% of the time.**

These trends weren't always about buying things either. They were telling me how to parent my children, feed my family or how to lose weight. And I used to take this information in from magazines, the internet or friends and think it was prescriptive. That I had to acknowledge and do the same because it was the best way. I also thought of it as an all-or-nothing thing so had to fully commit instead of just taking what resonated.

AWARENESS

I'm telling you about how I used to think and value things because I hope you'll get a better understanding of the place I am in now compared to where I was. I want to help you use the contents of this book to recognise the things that serve you truthfully and authentically so you can use that feeling to continue to make good decisions and choices. Having that awareness is the key to growth, because we all make mistakes but with awareness we can reflect and move forwards.

This is also how I want you to assess what you want in your home. It's not a case of looking at what others have and thinking that if it works for them, the same will happen to you if you have the same. Ask yourself if, when you do it, something gives you sufficient After Value to continue doing it and to feel the lasting effects?

Does any of this sound familiar? Are you living your life for other people, putting others ahead of yourself, spending money on things that don't make you happy?

Fast forward to Arthur being born and how I changed my perspective on life.

TAKING CHARGE

When I was pregnant with Arthur, I assessed my 11 years with George and decided to make some changes this time around. We were not planning any more children after Arthur and with me being 11 years older and in a much more secure and loving place in my life, I wanted to have a go at doing some of the things I felt myself and George missed out on. I wanted to set some goals that made me happy and were a far cry from everything you have just read about how I used to think.

Some of the things on my list were:

I wanted to have a financially secure year off work with Arthur: George was also going into the last year of primary school so I really wanted to use the time to be able to do pick-ups and drop-offs with him to give him a year off from going to breakfast and after-school clubs. This meant I had to stop buying all that 'stuff' from before, because this time I planned to save the money to help me stay off work longer.

I wanted to go to a baby group: I did go to one baby group with George but I was a 21-year-old in a group with what seemed like very confident mumsy mums talking about how much salt was in the baby food from the supermarket. I was so panicked and insecure back then that I went home and made all George's food from scratch for a long time, certainly for the whole weaning stage. And I really think it is amazing and perfectly brilliant that I did this, but in some situations a jar of baby food is needed, you know?

The goal here was to go to these groups with my own parenting choices that I was proud of and not change them because I thought people would like me more if I behaved more like them. No more people pleasing. I wanted to make friends and let Arthur socialise with his peers. This is exactly what happened and I had a great time in these groups and am still in contact with a couple of the mums and dads I met.

I wanted to practise my cooking: I have always loved cooking and baking but am not a natural and could never prioritise it over other tasks to get better. I wanted to make good, healthy food for the kids, Jacob and myself. Cooking and baking was always something I thought I didn't have time for and now I was going to make it more of a priority. This goal will always be a work in progress though!

I wanted to experience the stay-at-home-mum life: I absolutely love working, but I know it was the reason I missed out on things in George's childhood, the reason I was stressed and moody some days and the reason I didn't see him much at events like Christmas (in retail we work till Christmas Eve and then are back in again on Boxing Day). I think I saw George's Christmas play once, and that was because I lumped all my lunch breaks together and my friend Tori drove me right up outside school and then dropped me back at work after.

George also hated breakfast and after-school clubs but it was a no-choice situation, and I was excited for these things to become a choice for the first time. When I reflect back on this now I think this was more of a goal to allow me to slow down and have some space to think about what I really wanted to do with my life. I wasn't happy in my current job and I missed life at the store, but I didn't want to go back so it gave me time and space to think about what my next steps were. And although I didn't leave my job, I did go back part-time, which was such a huge help for me at that point in my life. We had less money with me being part-time but as a family we were much happier and it brought After Value to us. I loved working and I loved having more time at home, so it was a win-win situation and the drop in money was worth it.

PLANNING AHEAD

While I was on maternity leave doing all of these things, I was also trying to lose the four stone of baby weight I'd put on. I really struggled with my body and mind while pregnant with Arthur. I had reflux which I ate my way through, and so much water weight that towards the end I swelled so badly I had to wear Jacob's shoes to work one day (and they felt so bad for me they sent me home). I was ill for the whole pregnancy and it was just devastating to me as I wanted to experience that glow everyone talks about in my last pregnancy but I didn't.

At 35 weeks we were told Arthur wasn't growing at the rate he should be, and I was induced at 37 weeks with Arthur weighing a very cute 5lbs on the dot. When he came out, I can't explain to you the fire inside me – to feel good about my body, to get my mind back on track, to enjoy my year off to the fullest. If I hadn't taken that year off and worked on myself, I probably wouldn't be writing this book. And you would be reading a simple folding guide that told you to do it my way because it just looks really good. I am so grateful for that year as it shaped and evolved my philosophy to make decisions for my life and my goals determined on that After Value.

SURROUND YOURSELF WITH POSITIVE MESSAGES

I remember the first thing I did when I got home after the birth was to go to my Instagram and unfollow accounts that would make me feel bad about my body, and any parenting accounts that could make me feel like I wasn't a good enough parent. And let me just say this isn't because these accounts were posting anything with the intention of making me feel bad, but I was protecting myself because I knew I would feel bad watching their posts and comparing myself to them.

I decided to surround myself on social media with accounts that were positive, educational and made me feel good. I started following people like Megan Rose Lane, The Completion Coach; I went to one of their live workshops hosted with Becki Rabin and it was transformative in itself, and cooking and baking accounts led me to finding nutritionists' accounts that reflected my goals. My visits to social media became a lot more interesting, enjoyable and useful.

Next, I started walking. One thing we did to save money was sell one of our cars – Jacob worked from home and I was off so it made sense for that time in our lives. I started walking George to school with Arthur in the buggy. We'd leave the house at 8am and get there for 8:40am. George and I had 40 minutes of chatting and playing games on the way and then I'd tick off some errands on the way back at the shop and post office. And sometimes I'd stop for a chat if I saw a friend. As I walked back, I could put my headphones in and listen to a podcast if I wanted to. The whole journey was so much more than just a walk to school; it was peace, education, social interaction, a dose of fresh air, exercise – a good start to every day. I started to realise all of the benefits I was getting from the walking, and just the fact that I felt so good! I started walking at other times of the day too and planning activities that were more outdoors and involved getting active. I never went out as much with George but now with Arthur we go out for a walk at least once a day. The good feeling I had and how my mood lifted – these boosts were what I now describe as After Value.

"

The good feeling I had
and how my mood lifted
– these boosts were
what I now describe as
After Value.

"

ATTRACTING CHANGE

With all these changes happening in my life I really started to realise what made me happy and what didn't. I believed that my own happiness was worthy of coming first. But most important of all, I started to understand that by taking care of me first, everything else was falling into place naturally. The things I'd worked so hard to accomplish and the time I thought I didn't have and the things I thought I couldn't do *were happening*. Then one day I watched *The Secret* on Netflix and it all made perfect sense. The 'laws of attraction' were making things happen for me. I was surrounding myself with things that would encourage me to be the person I wanted to be, and the After Value was wonderful.

I began assessing my life using this new currency of After Value. It wasn't a formal thing, I just started doing it naturally in response to these new experiences I was having. The name actually came one day when I was trying to explain it to my followers.

> **"**
> **I believed that my own happiness was worthy of coming first.**
> **"**

The feeling of After Value is a more valuable currency than money. The walk to school took up more time and meant we had to get up earlier, but weighed up with all those benefits I listed earlier and the After Value made it worth doing. It's the same with my folding. I like folding clothes as I find the action itself therapeutic, but that's not the reason I do it. I do it because of the huge After Value it brings to my home. And I have to say there are so many situations that still crop up where I think, 'Wow, if I hadn't folded those clothes, that wouldn't have gone so smoothly.' The folding or small task is a present to your future, chaotic self.

Let's take a newborn baby as an example. When Arthur was born I had all his baby grows lined up in SKUBBs in his drawers, all folded nicely. I also had the most organised nappy area in an old footstool in the living room. If an 'explosion' happened, there was no panic. Due to my organisation, I could easily, and one-handedly, grab all I needed in seconds, change him and settle him back down so I could continue watching *Game of*

> ## " I began assessing my life using this new currency of After Value. "

Thrones (this is what I watched in the weeks after I had him and I loved it). Whereas if I think back to George 12 years earlier, this scene may have been a bit more chaotic, and I certainly would have got stressed and broken a sweat. To add, back then if I had got stressed, I was in a place where I also would have let that ruin my whole day. It's all about setting yourself up for success.

It's this kind of situation, and the After Value I recognise, that gives me the motivation to keep organised. I'm not naturally organised; honestly! And when I'm not I hold only myself accountable (even if I blame Jacob sometimes) and work a little harder to get there, to push myself to keep it up.

But I know the more organised I am, the more After Value I create, and the easier and more content my life is for me and others around me. I will say though sometimes if things get messy it's a good reminder of why you are organised. At the moment, we're doing up the new house so we've had no choice but to let things go until it's all finished but we are excited to get this place organised again!

After Value is how I now decide what I do, what I buy, what I eat, who I spend my time with and where I go. And people often assume it has something to do with a price tag, but it really doesn't. There are expensive things I've stopped buying because of the low After Value (like silly amounts of shoes I wear only once), and then there are things I've been spending more money on, like higher-quality fresh food I know is going to taste better and be more nutritious. But the most pleasure I get is from the activities and choices that come for free – like folding clothes and organising a cupboard. The monetary value is totally irrelevant most of the time (unless something is going to put you in debt and you can't afford to pay it back, then that would damage the After Value).

MAKING HONEST DECISIONS

It's about thinking with an unconditioned mind. Don't follow what you think is the norm or what you've been brought up to believe in. Judge it with your own feelings first, in the present. Because it's about how you feel and no one else. Your After Value will be different from that of others, and that's okay. In fact that's how it should be! This is a fresh way of thinking, and although some things get to stay in your life, there are some new things you may find you just can't stop when you realise their After Value (like folding clothes). You might be like me and find out that walking and nature are your new passion over watching the Kardashians (although... I do still watch them now and again). Give in to what truly serves you, whatever that may be, without caring about the opinions of others. It'll be a journey to work all this out – but I hope this book encourages you to join me in this.

> **"**
> **I'm not naturally organised; honestly!**
> **"**

Every individual will have a different After Value because everyone is unique and lifestyles, priorities and dynamics are different in every home. What serves you well in your family may not serve someone in theirs. We must just focus on our own spaces and our personal After Value. We must also understand that although we want something to give us After Value, it might not be right for us. And that doesn't mean it will never be right but just not at this present time.

In summary, After Value comes when something or someone serves your life and the lives of those close to you. It's about having an awareness of that good feeling inside of you and making decisions based on keeping that good feeling alive! It will help you understand what truly makes you happy and what doesn't, allowing you to expel what's not working from your life and make your priorities 100% authentic. Recognising After Value will also help you respect different ways of life and stop you comparing yourself to others. You take control of your own happiness rather than waiting for others to improve it. Allow yourself to feel you are worthy of a happy, positive, purposeful and fulfilling life, filled with love and meaningful connections.

"

You take control
of your own
happiness rather
than waiting
for others to
improve it.

"

Here are some examples of things that give me high After Value and those that don't.

HIGH-AFTER-VALUE ITEMS / ACTIVITIES

Wire holder on my bedside table	Okay, so you may have seen this on my social media but this tiny, cheap little wire holder gives me so much After Value. It keeps the wires tidy and means I don't have to turn the light on to find the end of my charger. When we moved house it got lost and I did not enjoy life without it. I immediately ordered another and my After Value is back!
Walking	When I walk, I listen to a podcast and I am exercising while the fresh air makes me feel better. You get to pass your neighbours and say hello (some days when on maternity leave I felt like I spoke to no one so this always brought my vibrations up). Arthur would always have a great nap, and if he was awake he would enjoy watching the cars. He still loves a walk and if I get the pram out of the car, he runs to it, climbs straight in his seat and straps himself in. Walking has also made me more open to outdoor activities and this year we have started going on bike rides with Arthur in a toddler seat. I never did that kind of thing with George and now I don't know why.

Steak dinners	All of us love a steak. We have this thing where we 'rate the steak' that we've eaten. George gets a lot of After Value from going out for a steak dinner so it's a nice family thing we do, not often but we really enjoy it. A summer-holiday activity we did this year was go for a steak dinner 'lunch' and we had such a great time. There was more After Value in that for us than a day at Thorpe Park!
Reading	I get so much motivation and education from reading. I prefer non-fiction books but I have been mixing my genres and have realised the benefit of getting totally lost inside the story in a good fiction book. I love the feeling of not wanting to put a book down. I also love the conversations that come about from reading the same books as others. My gran is a big reader so it's something we have in common and can chat about. I love listening to other people's interpretations of books compared to mine too, and I also love reading books to the kids before bed. George hasn't taken to reading in his teenage years but Arthur loves to sit in his book corner and read.

LOW-AFTER-VALUE ITEMS / ACTIVITIES

Folding muslins	Folding muslins is one of my top requested folds and I understand why, we have loads of them and they are everywhere! For me, because Arthur is constantly using them and dirtying them, I find no After Value in folding them.
Going to the gym	I would love to say I find After Value from going to the gym, and I used to force myself to think I did because everyone else does. But I don't. I much prefer walking as exercise and the occasional group class. Every time I have joined the gym in the past I have started off well and then, when I've not felt the After Value, I've stopped going and have found alternative ways to move like walking.
Theme parks	They are okay. I'll go if I need to as part of a day out with others but the truth is they don't excite me and the kids aren't too fussed about them either. I used to think I was supposed to like them and so were my kids but they are just not our thing.
Sweets	Quite simply, I'm more of a chocolate person.

FIND YOUR AFTER VALUE

Why not draw up your own grid of high-and low- After-Value activities and items. Be honest about what really resonates with you. Look at what you currently do in your life, and what you want to be doing more of. Consider all aspects of your daily living – family, friends, work, hobbies and passions. Think back to moments of joy and success in the past and what they were about. Own your own wants and needs.

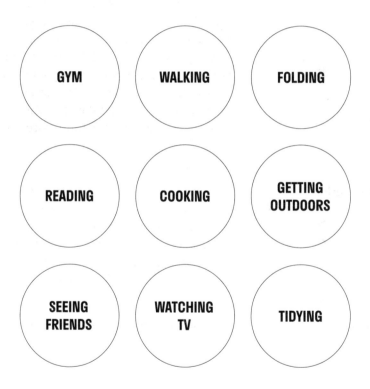

FINDING AFTER VALUE ON SOCIAL MEDIA

I felt it important to write about social media in this book because I have grown up in a world both with it and without it, so can make a fair comparison. I also had one baby without the presence of social media and then one with, so I use that comparison to remind myself of the effects it can have on parents, both positive and negative. And I have found myself using social media as part of my career. I have always loved social media and I feel like that's a bit of a dirty thing to say nowadays, but I do. I find it educational and inspirational, plus it's a big part of my career now, my communication medium from me to you. I have been on a journey with social media where in the past I have found it a negative space. But once I realised I was in control of what I saw, I understood how to make it a better place to visit.

The moment I realised that social media was bringing down my feelings towards myself, making me buy things I didn't get any After Value from and strive for things that I didn't really want making me doubt my values, I had a thought. . . Is it social media doing this to me or are there actions I can take to improve the situation? Social media didn't click 'buy' for me or say, 'Sophie, you must paint your house grey!' I was letting my mind be conditioned by what was being shown to me. And when I came to accept it was me allowing it to happen and I couldn't use people's accounts as an excuse, that's when my social media use changed for the better. Because I knew I had to take action myself. For myself. Because these accounts weren't going to stop posting things that made me spend money or feel like crap. It was up to me.

> **"**
> **Social media accounts weren't going to stop posting things that made me spend money or feel like crap. It was up to me.**
> **"**

We've all seen a picture of a home on social media and wished it was ours. We've also all purchased something we've seen in a home on social media to try to make our space more like that home. I read about 'Junk Values' in Johann Hari's book *Lost*

Connections: Uncovering the real causes of depression – and the unexpected solutions (Bloomsbury, 2018), where he explained that shorter relationships come from materialism. And this is certainly true with purchases made from wanting to be more like another person. We are looking for that connection to the celebrity world or some other life, without thinking about whether that product is right for our authentic selves or would actually suit our lifestyles. And that connection doesn't come because we didn't buy with After Value in mind; we bought with our Junk Values. Think about those purchases you made from seeing something on social media. How many have you got that you still use, and that have made a difference in your life? I bet not many at all have stayed around.

> **This is why we end up with so much stuff. So much that our homes seem small when they are actually the correct size for us.**

Junk Values are driven by a materialistic need for 'what they've got', a feeling that if you have it too you will be bigger, better and more important and connected. The problem is that feeling is there in the moment when you buy it, but it doesn't last afterwards. And then that feeling turns into regret at wasting your money, frustration when trying to keep your home tidy while you've accumulated all of this stuff you don't use in an effort to be something different, and sadness that the connection you thought you'd get wasn't actually there and didn't come.

And remember – this didn't start on social media; marketing is nothing new. TV ads, packaging, product placement, sponsorships and billboards have been around for decades, feeding our minds with messages of what we need in our lives. This is why we end up with so much stuff. So much that our homes seem small when they are actually the correct size for us.

When you turn these values around you will notice that stuff slowly starts to go and you open your home up to be a space that serves every person living there for what they really need it for. The time you used to spend constantly sorting out and tidying away will be less and that time can be used up on more worthwhile activities.

So my social media spaces are really positive, educational places. Are yours? See opposite for all my tips for turning your social media into a positive space!

It's critical that you turn off all your notifications so that you have to physically go into your app to find out what's going on. This was the biggest game-changer for me and something I did way before my career on social media. I now only have notifications turned on for one app and that is WhatsApp. All the rest have been turned off.

1.
Unfollow accounts that bring your mood down and give you bad thoughts about yourself and others around you.

2.
Follow accounts with content that truly interests you.

3.
Follow accounts with content you want to do more of.

4.
Do not photoshop your own content.

5.
Post your authentic self.

6.
Do not engage with negative comments.

7.
Do not comment if it's not supportive.

8.
Share your friends' and family's posts.

9.
Follow a couple of accounts that only post positive quotes.

10.
Follow people who inspire you.

AFTER VALUE
FOR CHANGE

Your home should be your favourite place to be. It's where you relax, work, play, socialise, eat, get creative, build relationships, make memories and everything else. It's your hub, your platform and your common ground with others. Your home should educate, encourage and inspire everyone in it. I have learnt more and more over the years about how important the home set-up can be to encourage the lifestyle you want.

If something is set up right in the kitchen, for example, you could become a master baker in a way you never would have been otherwise. Throughout the folding guide you will notice different set-ups around the home – for example folded clothes and the reading corner... These are all designed to make our routines easier and to encourage healthier behaviours that I know are important for a happy life.

I recently read a book by Dan Buettner called *The Blue Zones: Lessons for living longer from the people who've lived the longest* (National Geographic, 2008). This book visited the places around the world that recorded the most centenarians and studied their way of life to look for the connections we could learn from. Some of these places were Loma Linda in California, Sardinia in Italy and Okinawa in Japan, and when visiting and spending time with the people in these completely different countries the author found nine commonalities:

1. Move naturally – allow your everyday routines to make you move more
2. Purpose – wake up every day knowing your sense of purpose
3. Down shift – do things that lower your stress levels
4. 80% rule – stop eating when your stomach is 80% full
5. Plant slant – have lots of beans and lentils in your diet
6. Wine @ 5 – I will allow you to do your own research for this one!
7. Belong – have a sense of family, faith or/and community
8. Loved ones first – put family first
9. Right tribe – surround yourself with people who support healthy behaviours

Then, after reading Matthew Walker's *Why We Sleep: The new science of sleep and dreams* (Penguin, 2018), I added another important health need to my list:

- Quality sleep

And finally, I added in my own:

- Reading books/self-education

All of these are part of what influences my folding and organising guide. What encouraged me when reading about these people all over the world is that they genuinely did all live different lives yet still had these lifestyle factors in common that made them live longer.

> **"**
> **Factoring long-term tasks into your daily and weekly routine is so important to make them sustainable.**
> **"**

I realised the most important point about these connecting factors was that they were all part of the inhabitants' lifestyles and daily routines. And this is where I *always* fall down, and I am sure a lot of you will relate. . . I used to see, hear or read about something that was meant to be 'life-changing' and decided to make it part of my life, like the numerous diets I tried thinking they were the way to lose weight. I would struggle day by day, making sure I followed the plan, spend stupid money to get all the bits and equipment to get started, all the while not asking myself: 'Is this something that could be part of my lifestyle, my routine?' Or 'How do I make this part of my routine?' 'Is this something I will actually enjoy or do I just want the end result?'

Because this planning was never thought about, other priorities would naturally take over and that new action that was going to 'change my life' would quickly be a thing of the past. Then I'd be left feeling like I could never achieve what I wanted to and that I'd failed. Factoring long-term tasks into your daily and weekly routine is so important to make them sustainable. That's why the centenarians I had read about had maintained these commonalities throughout their lives.

MAKING THINGS HAPPEN

Then I thought about what allows for good routines and I listed the following:

- When things are easy
- When others hold me accountable
- When they are easily accessible or in my home
- When I constantly see them
- When I'm constantly talking about them

That last point about constantly talking about them is something I learnt from the Store Manager, Linda. We used to have a brief manager's meeting every morning and one thing we spoke about was loyalty cards.

> **"**
> **If we stop talking about it, we stop doing it.**
> **"**

How many had been given out, which department was doing the best, which was doing the worst... Every morning was the same chat and it was so boring. It wasn't our most exciting KPI (key performance indicator). Someone mentioned one day that the loyalty-card chat seemed like a pointless conversation adding no value. Linda just said, 'If we stop talking about it, we stop doing it.' And OMG, you know when someone just says something, and you have a 'that's so true!' moment. It was so simple, yet genius. It's the one quote that I remind myself of all the time. And sure enough, on the days she wasn't in and we maybe gave ourselves a break from talking about it we just didn't deliver. There was zero accountability.

HELP FROM YOUR ENVIRONMENT

This was when I started thinking about how I could set up my home to help me easily make these things part of my lifestyle without even trying – set myself up for success. Remembering my time working in the store, we didn't sell our products from the stock room, we sold them from beautiful displays on the shop floor that customers were attracted to, that gave them inspiration for their home décor or their Saturday-night outfit. When it was winter, we changed the stock to coats, hats and gloves. In summer we would display attractive picnic wear. We would encourage you to buy products we thought you needed, and you bought them and, I hate to say it, peeps, but you bought them easily! We marketed to you what we wanted you to buy through the way we set up and merchandised the store and now I'm saying let's set up our homes and market to ourselves the lives we want to lead, easily!

LET YOUR HOME DO THE HARD WORK

So in the store we showed you the things that we wanted you to buy and now you need to uncondition your mind and think about what you want your home to encourage you to do. Write down a few things. They could be long term or short term: short-term routines will relate to parts of life that are super-important to make easy and seamless, but that do have an end point – perhaps like changing a nappy or work/creative projects.

Then there are long-term routines that would benefit us as individuals if we carried on doing them throughout our lives – for example, eating nuts and seeds, drinking more water, having a good skincare routine and getting quality sleep. What are your priorities and how can your space support and enable them? Start your list.

MY DAILY ROUTINE

Be specific in your goals. Here are examples of some of the ones I'm currently working on and what I did to make sure my home is set up to cement them into my daily routine:

I WANT TO. . .	HOW TO ARRANGE THE HOME TO MAKE IT HAPPEN
. . .drink a green juice every day because I believe it will improve my vitamin intake and give me more energy as I've been feeling sluggish lately.	**Easy** – all the tools are out and ready to go, no set-up required **See it** – on the countertop **Talk about it** – I can see it so my brain talks about it every time I see it **In my home** – I bought everything I needed and set it up in my home
. . .put a wash on every day and the reason I want to do this is to keep on top of the laundry pile.	**Easy** – the laundry care is in the cupboard next to the machines and always fully stocked with easy-open jars and scoops **See it** – the set-up is in my kitchen so there's no hiding from it. I also don't have laundry baskets in the bedroom because they get hidden and forgotten about **Talk about it** – I see it there so my brain talks about it **In my home** – I bought everything I needed and put it in my home

Do you see how much detail I go into?
Particularly with the 'making it happen' bit.

FOCUS ON TIME-SAVING

'Retail is detail', as my manager, Linda, used to say. But give yourself a break. We live in a world now where time is precious and it's not that we don't have the time, it's largely because we waste time on the little things we don't have to or want to be doing. We also waste a lot of time procrastinating because we don't want to do tasks, so having them set up to be quick and easy will help you get your arse into gear. Set yourself up for success! Once the areas in question are arranged properly, your home will naturally encourage and motivate you to action those routines.

> **Set yourself up for success! Once the areas in question are arranged properly, your home will naturally encourage and motivate you to action those routines.**

PATIENCE IS A VIRTUE

The other thing I think we are guilty of is 'wanting it all and wanting it all now'. We're trying to eat healthily, fold all our laundry, get quality sleep, etc. all in one hit! You can have it all but if you want it to be sustainable you can't have it all right now. To make something a lifestyle habit requires patience and practice. Slow and steady wins the race. Write down some aims and think about the actions that are realistic for where you are in your life.

When I said I wanted my home to encourage me to read more, I decided I was going to set up an area to read in. I didn't just click my fingers and then the area was complete. I spent a few months sitting on chairs testing for the correct one. Finding shelves. Then I sat in the chair for the first time and realised I needed a little table for my cup of tea. And I spent another month finding that and saving for it. Then, once the area is finished, you have to allow those behaviours to manifest. And believe me they will, because you've set up a space to encourage it, ready to serve you with After Value. Your home is starting to work for you on your terms, to encourage the lifestyle you want to live.

***

I want to close this section with the important reminder that these actions you want to encourage must be authentic to you, not something you've seen on social media and want to copy. They should be something you have a real reason for wanting, that you think you can fit into your lifestyle at this point in your life. If they're Junk Values, these routines will not happen. Recognise that After Value to successfully implement these routines.

"

To make something
a lifestyle habit
requires patience and
practice. Slow and
steady wins the race.

"

HOW TO RESET YOUR SPACE

Before we get to the folding guide, where I share my most transformative folds with you, I first want to take you through my RESET process: the set of points I always consider when resetting, or changing and improving a space, big or small. It's quick and easy to integrate into your organising and something you can think about or write down if you prefer. Use this however it suits you and I promise it will help you to improve your space so that your home becomes more functional, is considerate of everyone using it and, most importantly, is quick to tidy up!

WHAT IS A RESET?

First though, I want to explain my thought process when I RESET a space. I call this a reset because the definition fits the task perfectly. The definition of reset is *'to set, adjust, or fix in a new or different way'.*

It's not always about getting rid of everything you're doing already, purging lots of clutter and making whole-scale changes. It can be just about adjusting and tweaking and trying something new to solve a problem, to reach a more meaningful end goal, to fix a priority. Whether small or large, the word 'reset' seems to fit all instances and reminds us that this organising of our homes and lives is something that continues forever because life evolves, people evolve, families evolve and a reset will always be relevant.

THE RESET

The RESET is a cycle I have put together which reflects my thought process when I reset a space. This is a set of values that I recognise as important in making organising and tidying meaningful and, therefore, sustainable.

If you dive straight in and organise a space you will achieve something, but you may not have fully considered who is using this space and why, or the resources you could have used. You might not have given yourself time to reflect on: 'Does what I've done work?'

These thoughts I have written down for you will help you prepare your resources, be more thoughtful and considerate to others and really achieve something that is going to work well in your space with your home dynamics.

There are five elements to the RESET:

1. **R**ecognise
2. **E**ngage
3. **S**et-up
4. **E**xecute
5. **T**est

Much of what you do within each element will be personal to you, so take everything I say as inspiration, not a prescription. Read the principles and relate them to your own environment, lifestyle and the people in it. You are the leader of the RESET but others will need to get involved at certain stages.

You may recognise your whole home needs a RESET, but please break this down into small spaces and apply the five elements to each project – a wardrobe, a room or even one single drawer. This will keep you motivated to regularly recognise resets that need to happen and help you prioritise your time to get them done.

THE HOME CYCLE

Before we get into each element, I want to share this thought with you. . . housework is never-ending. Not only because we as humans are constantly using things in our home, but because we are constantly evolving as we learn and grow. Because of this our interests change and what we want for our lives changes, and that means that what we have in our homes and how they need to function will inevitably change.

Therefore, you need to get rid of the expectation that you are creating a permanent solution to mess. A permanent solution to mess would be to not have any 'things' or, if we had things, not to let anyone touch them, and that would be a sad world to live in. Mess is such an amazing thing we should be grateful for. It can be the sign of a good play time, the result of a good meal, the aftermath of an amazing family party or the result of the perfect day off.

What we want is mess that stays just as that – a sign of a good time. We want to aim for mess that is easy and quick to tidy up, and not overwhelming or out of control. The tidying-up part needs to be enjoyable and requiring no major motivation to start. Look on it as a few moments where you can put some music or a podcast on and put everything away, rather than this chore that everyone avoids. And all that is achievable with a little bit of meaningful organisation, which we will get into now (and in each section I have written a case study that will help you relate it to home life).

R – RECOGNISE

The first part of RESET – **Recognise** – is about *feeling* the trigger for change. The trigger could be a positive or negative one. Why do you want to reset the space – is there a recurring argument about where something is, or perhaps a new baby is on the way or a bedroom swap is necessary?

By feeling the trigger first, we give purpose to our action. It gives us the *why* to what we are doing. When you think about the why and find your purpose, then your planning will be much more considerate and you are more likely to meet your goal. Remember, this is not 'because I saw she had it on social media' – that may be your inspiration but should not be your goal.

We often jump straight into things without thinking them through or being fully prepared. The reasons why we might do this are when:

- We are triggered by something online
- We are not using After Value as an assessment of why we're doing it
- We haven't given ourselves enough time before a deadline
- We are spontaneous by nature
- We just feel motivated in the moment

"

Mess is such an amazing thing we should be grateful for. It can be the sign of a good play time, the result of a good meal, the aftermath of an amazing family party or the result of the perfect day off.

"

There are three main reasons for recognising that a RESET needs to happen:

1.   **Something has come to an end:** Your space is now open to something new. This is a less urgent situation so you can really take your time thinking about what that change could be. This may mean you have gained space and can spread out a bit, be a little more indulgent and really work with the aesthetically pleasing side of organising. It could mean you now have room for that hobby you always wanted to do. This could also have a big knock-on effect to resetting the rest of the house so be ready for that now you have more space.

Examples could be:

- A child moving out
- Going back to work after working from home
- A relationship ending

2.   **New beginnings:** New beginnings usually mean additional space is needed/something is being added to your home. This may mean you will need to reset other areas in order to make additional space, perhaps adapting and working out priorities within the home. This is an addition to the home rather than a change so will possibly encompass a lot of space-saving ideas, letting go of some belongings and buying some practical items to help with the organising.

Examples could be:

- New baby
- New pet
- Working from home

3. **Change is needed:** This is different to the first two categories as it often starts with a negative emotion or annoyance. But it can also be something you recognise needs improving to make a space work harder for you. This is the most common start to a RESET and one you will come across more than the other two.

    The trigger for this may cause a lot of distress, not just for the argument it causes but for the aftermath of negative energy it leaves afterwards. Resetting for change is such a positive action and the great thing is that improvement is often immediate. These resets are started with the intrinsic motivation to improve the energy in the space and the After Value of these resets are sky high!

Examples could be:

- Everyone is late out of the house every morning because they can't find keys/bag/coat
- You are not motivated to cook because you can never find any ingredients
- Your toddler is constantly asking you to grab their books/ toys because they cannot reach them

What these three reasons have in common is that from start to finish the space stays the same. The only thing we change are the things within it.

CELEBRATE YOUR SPACE

People so often say to me 'my house is too small', 'but I only have shelves', or 'my bedroom is never tidy' as if they wished they had something else. But starting from now you must not do this. You should appreciate your home whatever it looks like or has to offer. It is your space, your sanctuary and the place where your memories are made. Whatever you have, we can make it work.

You can't change the size of a space, but you can work out how to cater for it and get realistic! You could buy a new wardrobe or some drawer dividers but this will never be enough for you if you continue thinking that it's too small. It's not too small, it just needs a reset to make it work harder for you.

> **One of the main quotes that I live by is: 'The definition of insanity is doing the same thing over and over again and expecting different results.'**

Relying on external motivation, like only reading my book, will not be enough for you to execute a RESET in a way that will work for your home dynamics and therefore be practical and sustainable. It must come from the first-hand experiences you have in your home – someone leaving, someone joining, the time you are spending on things that you wish you didn't or a chaotic vibe that you wish wasn't there. When you have that emotional connection to the task ahead the motivation becomes intrinsic and:

1. You will start and finish the job.
2. Your approach will be a more considered one with excellent decision making and After Value.
3. Any work needed to sustain the RESET will naturally move up in your priority list without you feeling that you must make time you 'don't have'.

Again, I'm a fan of Jillian Michaels' line: 'You can look for external sources of motivation and that can catalyse a change, but it won't sustain one. It has to be from an internal desire.'

CASE STUDY – ORGANISING KEYS

So let me set the scene: it's morning and everyone is about to leave the house to go to work/school. The kids have their coats and shoes on, bags on their backs and the adults (let's call them Shelley and Dan) have all their work bags packed and ready to go. But where are the keys? Everyone was on time and then, all of a sudden, they are behind schedule because no one can find the car keys. Shelley and Dan start arguing about who had them last and the kids get upset because they might be late for school, and because this happens a *lot* of mornings.

Eventually the keys are found but while driving to work Shelley can't help thinking how unnecessary this is every morning. One set of keys is ruining what could be a really seamless morning routine. If she doesn't do something, then the problem will just continue and she doesn't want that, so she decides to talk to Dan, to see how he feels and decide on a specific place for the keys.

I have deliberately used a simple example for the case study because it is usually the little things that cause the most damage to your daily life or lifestyle. And I want you to realise you don't have to live like that. You can take action and change the record. Otherwise, how can you expect anything to change? One of the main quotes that I live by is: 'The definition of insanity is doing the same thing over and over again and expecting different results.' This is attributed to Albert Einstein passed to me by James Carpenter, my manager from the store.

Recognising when things need to change allows us to move forwards in ways that only brings more After Value than we expect. And you will see that as we move through this case study and revisit it in each section of the RESET process.

"

You should appreciate
your home whatever
it looks like or has
to offer. It is your space,
your sanctuary and
the place where your
memories are made.

"

E – ENGAGE

Engaging in effective communication about the RESET is key to it being executed successfully, and for the After Value to happen. As humans, we naturally feel the need to connect and communicate, and by engaging we can bridge that connection not only to the home and systems in place, but the people in it. Communication with yourself or the others that use that space before executing the RESET will create a more considered plan for the space itself. You also show your personal respect for those around you and the way they use the space.

The problem I see a lot of the time is that there is usually one person who enjoys or oversees all the tidying and organising. If you are that person, the reorganisation must happen with the wants and needs of the person or people using/benefiting from the space in mind, and not just your own. And we do this by simply engaging in a conversation or observing others' time in that space or reflecting on what we already know about the needs of those around us. When the organising is finished, the space will be released back to the owner. If the RESET has been meaningful and considerate, then we can trust it will be used correctly. And if other people can't use the RESET wisely, then it probably wasn't done with them in mind.

The communication I describe in this section applies to all types of spaces – offices, shared flats, or flats for one – but will be key for multi-functional/communal spaces. There is no limit on the people you should engage with. If you've realistically engaged with everyone, your planning will be successful. Remember, the more people you engage with, the more different wants and needs you may encounter. In that situation, work with the majority viewpoint and communicate to everyone that this was a necessary decision in order to move forwards.

Engaging questions could be:

- What would you like to keep?
- What do you use the most?
- What do you use that for?

- Would you like to change that?
- What do you think would help to enable you to do that?

From the answers to your questions you can then engage in some creative brainstorming of what you might need to buy or use from elsewhere around the home.

Engaging before a RESET can really help those people who find change difficult to process. Children, for example, often struggle with change, especially when it happens without them knowing. Their environment is important to them and it can cause frustration to a child when it is changed. Routine and consistency make a child feel secure, which in turn creates positive behaviours and independence. Giving children the opportunity to be a part of the RESET, even if it is simply to tell them that their room may change around, will prevent any negativity that could happen otherwise.

What I know from my TikTok audience in particular is that some young people do love to organise so you may even gain a helper, or they may want to do it themselves, taking the task away from you altogether. Woohoo!

The benefits of Engaging with others are:

- The problem is more likely to be solved.
- You are more understanding of others' needs.
- It shows you respect the way others choose to use a space.
- More clarity and direction around what is needed.
- It makes for a much more considered Set-up and Execution.
- Creativity is heightened.
- You may learn something about someone you didn't know, or realise that something is more important to someone than you thought.
- After Value is created.

CASE STUDY – ORGANISING KEYS

Shelley and Dan arrive back from work to the messy house they turned upside down when looking for the keys that morning. After a short conversation they agree that the keys need a home.

Dan and Shelley both make suggestions. Shelley wants to keep them in a pot by the door and Dan wants to keep them in a kitchen drawer. They decide to go with Dan's idea as he is very security conscious, hence him not being keen on keeping keys by the door. They also agree that Dan will pick the drawer and execute the RESET.

The final engagement needed is when the RESET is completed. You must walk the space together and discuss the changes that have been made. This way everyone can understand the system/s that have been put in place and can start to use them. When we do the handover to the owner of the space, we can also see this as a release. Sometimes if we put a lot of time and effort into something we feel like we own it and don't like to see it messed up. By handing over the space, you not only increase the chance of the new system/s being used and maintained, but you release your own thoughts of owning it back to the actual owner.

This all sounds very formal but it's really not. A two-minute conversation, a simple observation or some time to reflect can be all it takes to really start a solid plan to make the space work its hardest for everyone.

S – SET-UP

So, you've recognised the space that needs a RESET and why. You've engaged everyone who uses the space so they know what your end goal is. Now we need to think about what is needed to set it up. There's nothing worse than starting a RESET and not being able to complete it because you must stop and go out to buy something necessary.

To understand what you may need, ask yourself the following question: 'What is one result I want to get out of this RESET?'

The answer will fall into one of these three categories:

- Aesthetically pleasing
- Practical/functional
- Space saving

The important thing to remember is that your answer is the *only* target that you should focus on achieving. Anything else should be seen as a bonus. It's easy to want all three categories to work but in some situations it's not possible, so choosing just one manages your expectations and keeps you focused on what's most important.

With this in mind, you can work out any resources you may need. For example, if your main goal is to save space by making four drawers of clothes fit into two drawers, then to be able to achieve this, you may need some drawer dividers. However, if your answer didn't fall into 'aesthetically pleasing', you could let go of buying the drawer dividers and just use the storage you already have. If you want to order drawer dividers, this will be a bonus to your RESET. Or it could be something you do in the future.

This isn't just a way of thinking for the Set-up but something you will need to continue into the Execute element as well. Sometimes the most practical action will not be the most space-saving or aesthetically pleasing, so we must always remind ourselves of our priority outcome to make peace with what has been achieved.

A little note about buying items: I do believe items such as drawer dividers are worthy of my money for the After Value they bring. But the cost can add up if you have a lot of drawers. I used to buy one box every time I got paid until I had enough. We might not be able to have it all straight away but that doesn't mean we can't do so over a period of time. The long game can bring the small wins together in the end!

There are several staples that I use in my home and would recommend. I will describe how to use them as we take the book around the home in Part 2:

- Drawer boxes/containers like the IKEA SKUBBs – (available in a pack of six in three different sizes).

- Drawer dividers – various ranges available from Amazon or The Container Store in the US.
- Glass jars – various types available from retailers or just reusing attractive ones once the contents have been used. I prefer glass containers in the kitchen because glass is easier to clean and I can run it through the dishwasher.
- Hangers – enough so that all your clothes are on matching hangers.
- Baskets – available from various retailers.

To save money and get super-savvy, recycle what you already have to use as your storage staples. I have seen my followers use shoe boxes, cardboard drawer dividers and jam jars as just a few very effective examples.

CASE STUDY – ORGANISING KEYS
Shelley chose a drawer in the kitchen which had a space for the keys and she found a spare bamboo drawer insert she could use. There was nothing else needed.

As part of the Set-up, make sure you have accounted for how long you might actually need. Plan time for the following:

- Start and finish (this could be an hour or three days, depending on the scale of the RESET).
- Pause/break – allow yourself a few breaks throughout the RESET to stop and assess what's going on, where you are up to, what still needs doing and in what order. Are you working towards your one goal? Take a rest if necessary.
- Tidy up – this time should be used to make the space liveable in if your RESET is going over a couple of days or if you are at the end, and getting rid of rubbish or purged items. It is important that this is part of your timing; do not make a mess in another part of the house with a project.

I find I stay motivated if I'm listening to a podcast or music. If the RESET is a long one, I will put something on Netflix, usually *Friends*, as I've seen it so many times it doesn't become a distraction but rather background noise. Plus, watching Monica can be very motivating!

E – EXECUTE

Let the games begin! This is where you do the physical work – resetting that wardrobe, drawer or bedroom, whatever you have planned. *Part 2: The Folding Guide* will give you the necessary skills for this stage but have some music, podcasts or audio books ready. Plus water, and maybe a snack. Enjoy yourself and get lost in this time because you are creating some incredible positive vibes for your home. This should be the fun bit!

HOW TO KNOW IF SOMETHING IS WORTH KEEPING

Now I wasn't sure where this section fits because I don't see purging as a set activity. Often there should be an initial throw-away session before a RESET begins, and this will help you understand what you need and how much space you may have. But also allow yourself to continue to purge throughout the Execution. Sometimes I find myself loving what the RESET is doing for the space and how good it feels, so much that I realise there are more things I don't need. Once I start to feel greater After Value from the space I am creating, this ability to assess what is and isn't needed can become easier.

But how do you know if you should keep something or not? The only question you need to ask yourself is: 'How much After Value does it give me?' If you really want to keep something, then please keep it! Just because you saw a stunning wardrobe online, housing just two jumpers and a pair of jeans, it doesn't mean this is what you should have too. I have one pair of black jeans and my sister has around 20. Imagine if I was organising her clothes and decided to throw out 19 pairs of her jeans, basing my decision on what was right for me and not her. She'd have no work clothes! So both amounts of jeans are correct because I do not wear black jeans often and she wears them every day for work. Do what works – find the meaning, the purpose and the After Value for you and decide. I'm not here to tell you you've got too much stuff; I'm here to help you recognise when you do. And also to help you fit everything you want into your space without it being overwhelming. And I trust in you that you will know.

There are ways to lessen your load without throwing something in the bin:

- Donate to charity
- Pass on to family member/friend
- Create a memory space in the loft
- Sell or give away for free online (eBay, Facebook marketplace, Gumtree)

Once you understand After Value, there is a big chance you'll have a look at your 'stuff' and know what you want to purge. You're going to have that moment where you recognise your home is your boundary and you've overbought for it, leaving you feeling stupid for ever saying 'I've got no space' or 'my home is too small'. When you begin to purge, I want you to know this can be a very uncomfortable exercise for most people. This is probably why you've been putting it off for so long. You are going to feel some of the following feelings:

- **Embarrassed** – that you spent so much money on things that you didn't use, need or want.
- **Horrified** – at how many clothes still have their price tags on them.
- **Upset** – when you recognise the monetary value of all the items could have been spent on a holiday or training course you said you couldn't afford.
- **Shocked** – at all the purchases you forgot about.
- **Annoyed** – that you have been complaining about not having enough space for all this time when the truth is... you overfilled your home.

But when you've finished you're also going to feel:

- **Relieved** – that the clutter has now gone.
- **Satisfied** – that you can now see all your belongings.
- **Love** – for the things you have chosen to keep and the good vibes they give you every time you look at them.

- **After Value** – for all those uncomfortable feelings you had to face to get to this point of organisation.

Your future purchases will now be made with After Value in mind. Your home is your boundary and space is good – you do not have to fill every nook and cranny. Remember all of this.

CASE STUDY – ORGANISING KEYS

Shelley put the bamboo drawer insert in the drawer in the kitchen and placed all the significant keys in it. She also added some labels to other keys, like the garage key and back door key to add to the organisation. She spent about half an hour on the job, 25 minutes of which was the extra labelling she added. She was so happy that all the keys in the house were nicely organised and felt good about this new system working. When she had finished, she showed Dan the drawer and where the keys were. She also showed the kids and told them if they see any keys lying around, then they must put them with the other keys in this drawer.

T – TEST

As you know I give my RESETs a test period to show me they work for my home. For me it's around a month but sometimes I can tell straight away if it's not working. Usually if a RESET hasn't worked it's because I didn't make my main aim the priority. I might have got lost making things look aesthetically pleasing or tried to save so much space that the RESET wasn't practical. This can and does happen.

> **Take control of what you can in the chaos of the daily grind.**

If you find after a month that it's still not working for you, then RESET again. The difference this time is that it probably won't take up much of your time. You may just need to revisit the Set-up element, maybe order some baskets or spread things out a bit more or part with a few more things. Ultimately, the work that you put into the first RESET will not be wasted and you'll have a much better idea of what you need to do this time. Some areas are about trial and error. You know the RESET is working perfectly when you forget about the testing period!

CASE STUDY – ORGANISING KEYS

Around three weeks after the keys RESET, Dan had a moment of reflection one morning, when he turned to Shelley and said, 'Have you noticed leaving the house has been seamless the last few weeks? What's changed?' Shelley laughed and replied, 'Remember – we moved the keys?' Dan had totally forgotten because it was such a small problem to solve but the realisation of the massive change it had made amazed him.

I purposely used something as small as moving keys as the example for the RESET case study to show you this isn't always about massive room or house sort-outs. This is also about the little things in life having major positive effects. In the world right now it seems only big and fast are relevant, but I believe slow and small can have a big impact on our lives. That's why when you do RESETs round your home, break it down and don't miss the small RESETs.

PART 2

THE
FOLDING
GUIDE

TO START WITH

This is it – the Folding Guide! I am so excited for you to be reading this, and for what will happen once you have. I am about to share with you my most transformative folds, the folds that my followers have found the most After Value in using. We're going to move around the home, room by room, and I will take you through my favourite folds for each space and share my organising hints, tips and hacks. We'll look at folds for all of your clothing (plus any children's) in the Bedroom section along with how to handle bedding; then we'll fold towels and flannels in the Bathroom section, and cloths and napkins in the Kitchen section. Packing for Travel will help max out your space efficiency when travelling, and my favourite folds in the Gift Wrapping section will bring immense After Value to your present wrapping.

SETTING BOUNDARIES

Before we start folding, I wanted to tell you that I used to ignore all the pointless stuff I had accumulated in the flat because I couldn't bear to admit I'd wasted my money on it. I will not let you do the same!

When it comes down to it there are only two reasons to be unorganised:

1. You don't have the right storage system yet; or
2. you have too much stuff for the space you are in right now.

To understand which is your problem, you need to work through reason one to know if the answer is reason two. Know too that reason two isn't saying that the things you have are not needed or great purchases; number two is telling you that right now you have a set amount of space and you've overfilled it.

When you do your purges and RESETs, I want you to follow the rule of Boundaries. You should assign everything its own area, then assess how much of each category you keep. Use this to guide decisions you make about adding to that category in the future. For example, let's take leggings – a popular request so I'm guessing a lot of you own them. I have at least five pairs and wear them daily. Think about a space where you want to keep them. This space needs to reflect your usage of leggings in terms of position and size. Once you have chosen your space, you might find you have to get rid of some pairs. Going forwards the rule for this space becomes that you cannot overfill it (unless something in life changes and your usage increases, then it's time for a RESET). If the storage space is full and you buy another pair, then you must purge a pair to release space. It's a simple approach to using space but an immediate way to balance your needs and the space you live in.

Setting this type of boundary brings immense After Value in how you shop going forwards. It's an easy way to prevent unnecessary impulse purchases and gives you a greater understanding of how you spend money. Obviously, it will have a positive effect on your bank balance too. Setting boundaries for your possessions has a much bigger effect than it first appears.

I talk about folding and organising to save space a lot but I don't want you to create space just so you can fit more stuff in. If you make space and you have enough stuff, spread it all out and give it room to breathe, or learn to enjoy the space for what it is... something that doesn't create overwhelming tasks! Okay, are we ready to fold now? Let's do this!

FOLDING KEY

Here, you'll find a handy key explaining what all the arrows and lines mean – you'll see the symbols are repeated on each fold though!

The sizes of the illustrations are all to scale, so if the image gets smaller it's because the item is getting smaller! You'll see how a pile of your items will look at the end of each fold.

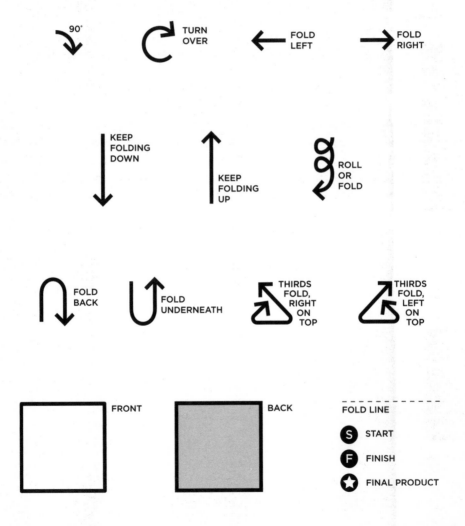

"

Now you're ready to get folding – let the journey begin. . . Make sure you mark this page and keep referring back to the folding key as you work through the folding steps!

"

SOME KEY FOLDS

Let's start with three of my main and most popular folds that can be used on so many items. If in doubt about which fold to use, try one of these; they work on everything from T-shirts to tea towels.

FOLDING INTO THIRDS

Thirds folding is my go-to for rectangular shapes, for example towels or sheets. I use my classic 'thirds and thirds again' fold to store my towels and then for larger rectangles I use it to end the fold. The best thing about using thirds is that it will keep your edges tidy, unlike folding in half. You have to try it to understand what I mean but we do lots of thirds folding throughout the folding guide.

Great for: rectangular items such as tea towels, bedding, bath towels and napkins.

THIRDS FOLD 1

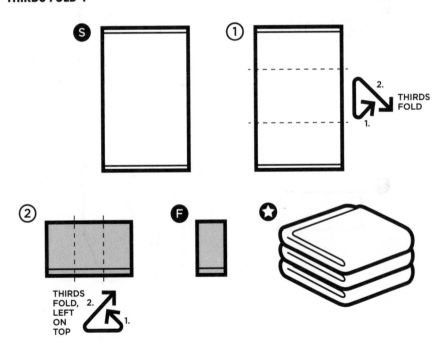

THIRDS FOLD 2

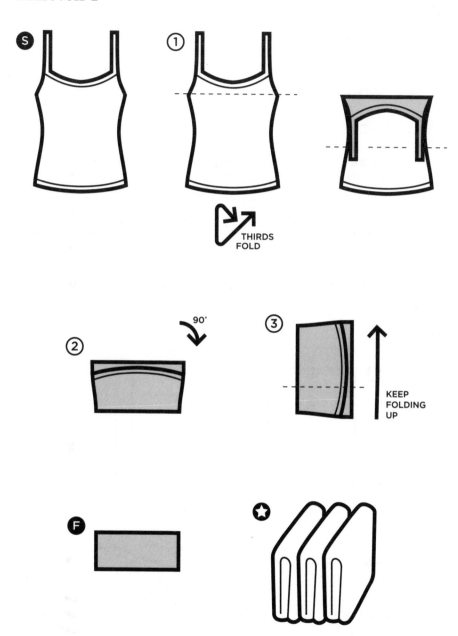

RANGER FOLD OR ROLL

The ranger roll originates from the Army, it's how they fold all their apparel to pack in their backpacks, as it saves space and keeps everything organised. I adapted this to include a fold too, which I love for blankets, towels and outfit packs.

Great for: towels, blankets and all clothing items for space saving packing.

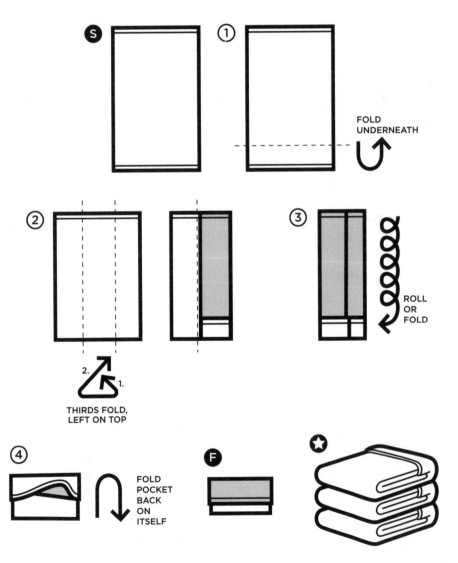

HALF FOLDING

This is so quick and easy, not always the most space saving but time saving. It's also great for very small clothing such as toddler and baby clothes, as smaller clothes are much harder to fold. I use this fold for football tops as the material is so flimsy and this gives it good form for storage. The fold ends with the badge showing, which is a bonus as it looks great in the drawer and aids selection for a messy teenager.

Great for: flimsy materials, football shirts, toddler and baby clothes, jeans and trousers

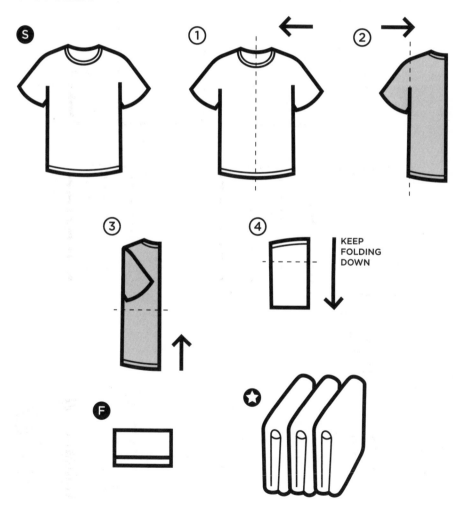

KEEP
FOLDING
DOWN

TIPS FOR FOLDING:

▶ Always leave a gap with your edges – this is what keeps your edges in check. Your edges will look neater if you always leave a gap.

▶ Start flat – where possible, it's always best to start the fold with your clothes as flat as possible. If your seams are all in place, then your fold will be easier and less wrinkly at the end.

▶ There's more than one fold for each item... the Test period will show you if it works for you.

▶ Adjust your fold for your space, not your space for your fold. It is much easier, practical and inexpensive in most circumstances to adjust the fold. For example, if the item is too big for the space, see if you can fold the sides in more to decrease the width.

▶ Think of the shape of your item and then you'll see that you can use the same folds for some of these items. Bedding, tea towels and tablecloths are all rectangles and the same folding technique could be used for all of them.

▶ Get rid of the straps or uneven edges in your first two folds, you should have a nice rectangle or square shape to end on.

▶ Give it time... it takes time to form a habit, find the After Value and the routine will naturally cement itself into your lifestyle.

▶ If you want to show the artwork on a piece of clothing, always start with your clothing facing down. Not all my key folds work for logos, but I'm sure you'll be able to make the adjustments if this is something that will bring you After Value.

There's no pressure or time frame, and this is definitely not an all-or-nothing guide. If you find the After Value in folding your jeans but not your underwear, that's fine! You must always take what resonates in the present and leave the rest. Again, we want to work on your space – to make the areas fit your priorities, filled only with what meets your needs (including the need for a beautiful space) and become easier to keep tidy on an every day basis – to soothe stress and help you feel that little bit more in control.

Start wherever you like. It's your home, so do pick and choose what works for you and where you need or want to begin. I am going to start in my favourite folding room. . . the bedroom!

BEDROOM

When you wake up in the morning this room is the first thing you see so it should set your mood to happy in order to start the day right. Think about it. What would you rather wake up to: a tidy bedroom where you can easily select your outfit for the day from your organised and tidy wardrobe/drawers, or would you prefer to step out of bed onto a pile of clothes and then spend 20 minutes looking for that top you wanted to wear? I'm hoping you preferred the first scenario!

A tidy, organised bedroom can really help that positive start to your day. If you recognise your bad mood being triggered by your bedroom in the morning, then it's time to consider a bedroom RESET. You should want to get out of bed in the morning because you know getting up and getting ready for the day ahead is going to be seamless and not negatively impact your day. And this applies to everyone – adults, children and guests. Don't underestimate the power of a tidy children's bedroom either, as environment can be a real mood setter for them. Let's have them wake up happy with the ability to get up, get dressed (if they are at that age) and leave their rooms raring to go... Agreed?

Whether it is an adult's, child's or guest bedroom, there are some fundamental actions that need to happen in the space:

- Sleeping
- Dressing
- Relaxing

These are the main things I suggest you focus on when starting your RESET or organisation. Any other considerations will be personal to the owner of the room and you will need to communicate and/or observe to understand what these are and make sure you include them in your Execute stage (of any RESET). This could include a homework, gaming, play or make-up area, to give you a few examples.

HANGING VS FOLDING

I always get asked: 'Which clothes should I fold and which should I hang? Does it matter?' And my answer always is... it all depends on your storage options in the space. Some rooms only have hanging areas, some have just a small or no hanging area. (Arthur and George now have only drawers so nothing in their rooms is hung.) Here are some ideas for you to consider:

- ▶ Everyday clothes – hang; make a capsule wardrobe of clothes you wear the most so all your regulars are accessible and in one place. This includes coats and jumpers you wear at that time of year and workwear. You could also add clothes you want to wear more. The more accessible the space, the more likely you are to wear the item of clothing.

- ▶ Gym clothes – fold; these generally do not crease as easily and are nice and compact when folded, so work better in a drawer.

- ▶ Coats and jackets – if not regularly worn I would fold these into a storage box and keep them in a less accessible part of the room, like the back of the wardrobe, under the bed or a cupboard space. Or consider moving them to the loft if you have that space. I would recommend airtight storage boxes or vacuum bags.

- ▶ Underwear and socks – no question, fold, although there are some lingerie options you may want to hang.

- ▶ Embellished or delicate clothes – hang these in a breathable bag so they do not damage any other clothes. You could also cut a small hole in an unwanted pillowcase and cover them with that.

Don't make the decision about whether to hang or to fold about space saving. The priority is ease of accessibility. Having your regular clothes hung in one place will save you much more time in the morning and also when putting the laundry away.

SHELVES GIVE SO MANY OPTIONS

I know shelving stresses a lot of you out, but I love shelves. They can give a space that luxurious shop feel and are a fantastic way to display really inspirational pieces, like the handbag you treasure or your fave jumper. I feel confident to call myself a shelf expert as the department store had a LOT of shelves, and at sale times we had to get a LOT of clothes on those shelves, so I am well-practised at piling high.

Shelves are great for all types of storage items, not just clothes, and I always advise that you start by assessing your shelf configuration. Would it be helpful to take out a shelf or add an extra one?

Why not treat your shelves like drawers – in two distinct ways:

▶ Work with shelves like open drawers – use open storage boxes such as the IKEA SKUBBs and use the same folds as you would for drawers (see below). If your storage boxes are not the exact size of your shelf and have space around them, don't look at it as dead space. Review the set-up as a whole, and ask 'Have I made the clothes accessible and the space user friendly?' It's okay to have some space. Leading me nicely to number two...

▶ Fold your clothes in piles. For this you are limited to the type of clothes you can fold – I don't recommend folding a pile of dresses or coats. But folding into piles is perfect for jumpers, jeans, T-shirts and hoodies. Once folded, piles look very satisfying too. Here are my top tips for folding piles of clothes:

▶ The flatter the fold, the higher the pile – try to do as few folds as possible keeping a larger surface area for the folded item.

- ► Try not to overlap your folds – this will make your clothes uneven and cause piles to topple.

- ► Size ordering looks great but keep in mind that accessibility should be your priority and make sure your most worn items are on the top of the pile. You'll move your pile to get to the bottom less then, so it is more likely to stay tidy.

- ► Try shelf dividers – with long shelves, shelf dividers can really help keep your piles in check. They are also useful for other types of storage; I use them in my work cupboard where I keep all my different types of storage boxes and they have allowed me to categorise what I have in stock and create some order.

FOLDING AND CREASES

If your clothes are folded and stored as per my folding guide you will have some light creases along fold lines (a fold is essentially a crease). Light creases and wrinkles usually fall out as the clothes are worn –your body heat make them drop out on wearing. It's the deep creases we want to avoid. Although, of course you can absolutely iron a piece of clothing before it's worn. Jacob is an 'ironer before he wears it'; he likes a freshly ironed shirt or jumper for work. It was Jacob who opened my eyes to the 'non-ironing after washing' world, as he irons clothing only just before wearing it, and I've never looked back...

There are some other causes of annoying creases so here are some tips to help prevent that happening:

- ► Fold clothes lightly... don't treat each fold like you're creasing a piece of paper. Keep it nice and loose.

- ► Don't pack the drawers or shelves too tight with clothes – the clothes will be squashed together and cause those deep creases that need ironing out. This also applies to hanging in the wardrobe. If you pack it all in, it will be more likely to crease.

▶ Avoid brands that crease easily. (I don't have any specialist information on specific materials because there's no way you'll find me checking labels of every item while I'm out shopping and there are so many variations of man-made materials, so I assess this by brand and feel.)

▶ Don't leave your clothes in the washer and dryer too long; ideally, take them out of the dryer when it's just finished and they're still warm. (Thank you to my #foldingfam on Instagram for that tip when I got my first dryer!)

▶ If you use a wash basket, don't pile the clothes up after they have just dried. The heavier the pile, the more pressure on the clothes and the deeper the creases. Try and form the habit of taking clothes off the line or out of the dryer and putting them where they go straight away.

▶ And lastly, keep up with the folding. Scrunched-up clothes in the drawer (or on the floor) are going to crease more than clothes nicely folded in a drawer.

ADULT BEDROOM

Let's start in the adult bedroom. The folds in adult's clothes differ from children's clothes as kids' clothes are so much smaller and options can be different. Remember that most of my folds can be applied to other types of clothing, so if I haven't demonstrated something here, then follow the basic principles for similar items of clothing.

FOLDING FOR SHELVES

My big rule with folding for shelves is making sure everything is all flat, flat, flat! If the folds are uneven, then your pile will topple over or not stack as high, and everything will not only look messy but will disorganise quickly.

You have two options for shelves. You can use containers into which you fold the clothes, as you would with drawers, and place those on the shelves. Or you can make vertical stacks that sit directly on the shelf.

For vertical stacks, the one product I recommend for long shelves are shelf dividers to keep the clothes in their compartments which, in turn, restrains any mess a pile can make. It also helps make the shelf look more cared for and curated and, as I mentioned earlier, the more pleasing it is on the eye, then the more motivated we are to keep it that way.

Let's start with our first fold – a simple T-shirt ready to sit on a shelf.

TIP
When stacking, put your least-used clothes on the bottom of the pile and your most-used towards the top. This makes your favourites more accessible and decreases the chance of mess.

T-SHIRT FOLD FOR SHELF

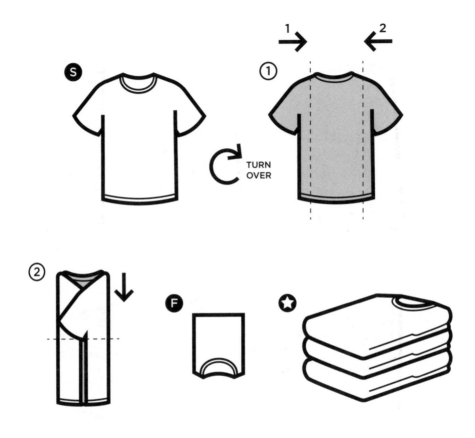

TIP
Using an A4 piece of paper or a
magazine as a size guide will help you
achieve the same width each time.

JEANS FOLD FOR SHELF

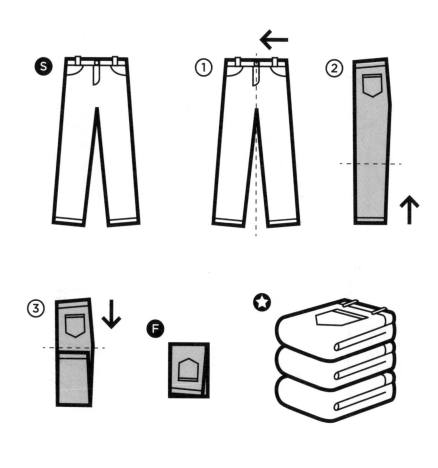

TIP
To make the pile narrower you can fold
in the crotch of the jeans during step 3.

HOODIE FOLD FOR SHELF

The fold for hoodies and sweaters is essentially the same fold, apart from the hood being an extra step for the hoodie.

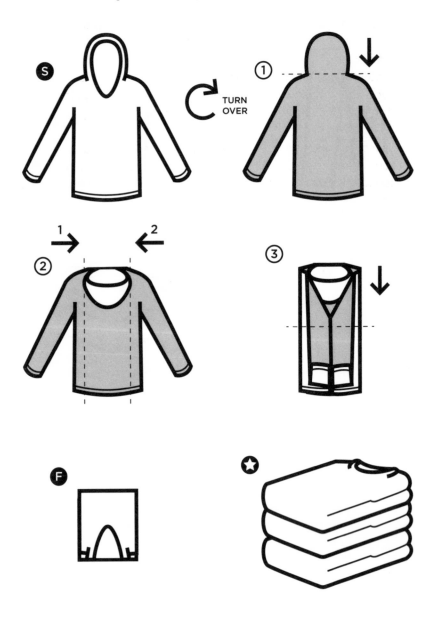

CHEST OF DRAWERS/DRESSER

Drawers can be a real space-saver. When we were in the flat and the boys had to share a room, we got rid of the wardrobe and bought them a chest of drawers each and the space we saved was unbelievable. Not only did we get all their clothes in them but we could also have a drawer for games and stationery, plus a football-only drawer for George.

To make the most of dresser space I use two main types of drawer dividers and storage. Extendable drawer dividers are great for larger items as you can choose the size of your section. Boxes are perfect for smaller items such as gym gear and baby clothes.

Amazon is a great place to buy the extendable drawer dividers, and I highly recommend the IKEA SKUBB range for boxes – they are a really good price to get you started. I warn you: once you buy your first pack of SKUBBs, you won't look back!

T-SHIRT FOLD FOR DRAWER

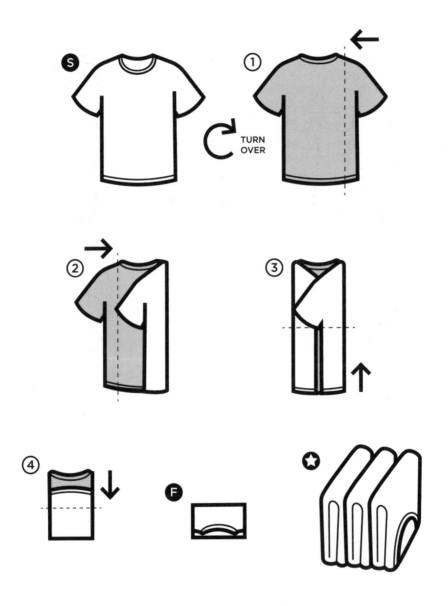

JEANS FOLD FOR DRAWER

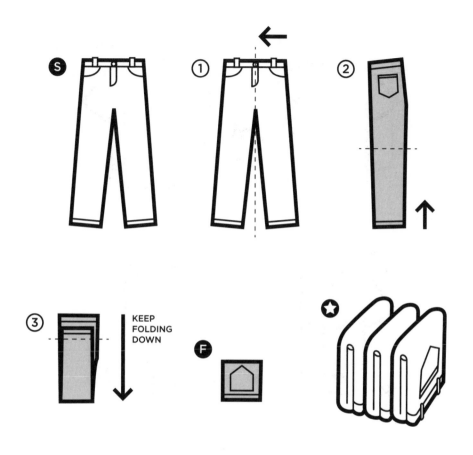

S

①

②

③ KEEP
FOLDING
DOWN

F

★

TIP
With drawers, put your most-worn clothes at the
front of the drawer; the more accessible they are,
the less mess you create and the more time
you save on selection.

JUMPER FOLD FOR DRAWER

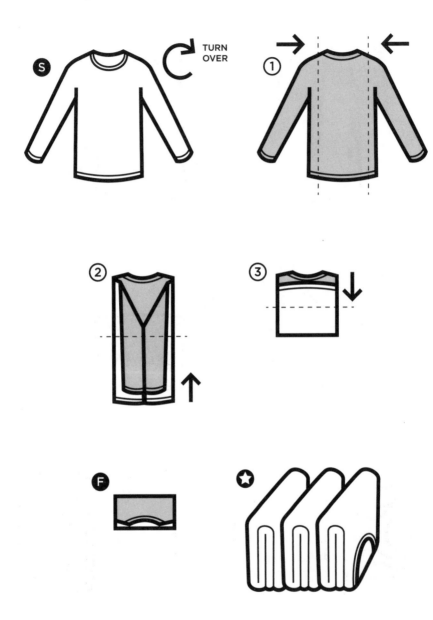

VEST TOP FOR DRAWER

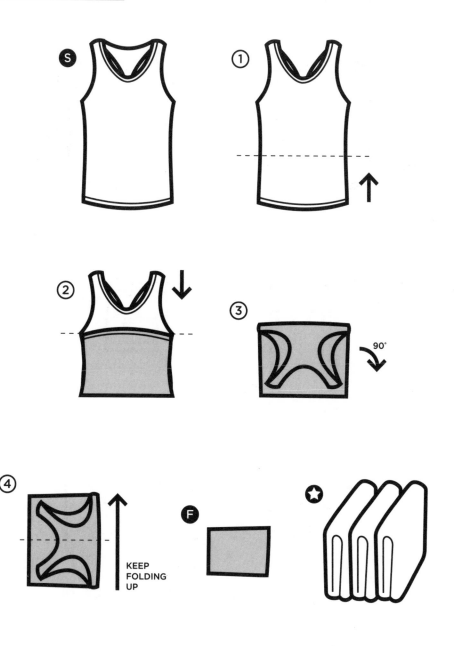

S

1

2

3   90°

4   KEEP
     FOLDING
     UP

F

★

LEGGINGS FOLD FOR DRAWER

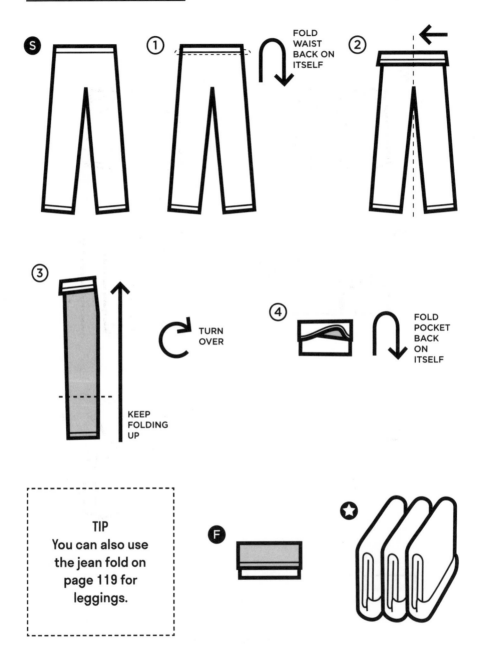

S

1 FOLD WAIST BACK ON ITSELF

2

3 KEEP FOLDING UP

TURN OVER

4 FOLD POCKET BACK ON ITSELF

TIP
You can also use the jean fold on page 119 for leggings.

F

⭐

SHORTS FOR DRAWER

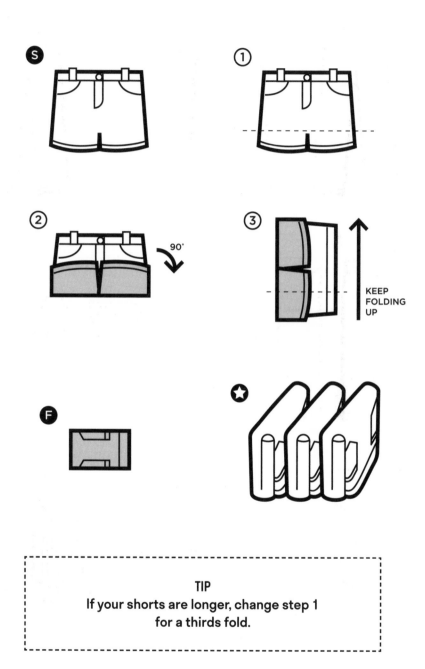

TIP
If your shorts are longer, change step 1
for a thirds fold.

UNDERWEAR

BOXERS

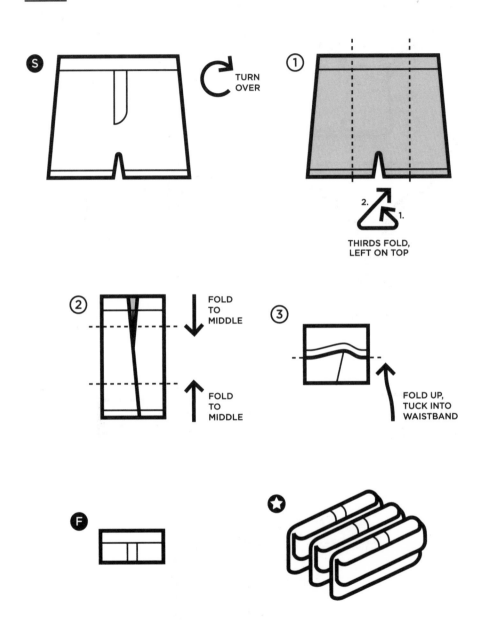

S — TURN OVER

1 — THIRDS FOLD, LEFT ON TOP — 1. 2.

2 — FOLD TO MIDDLE — FOLD TO MIDDLE

3 — FOLD UP, TUCK INTO WAISTBAND

F

KNICKERS

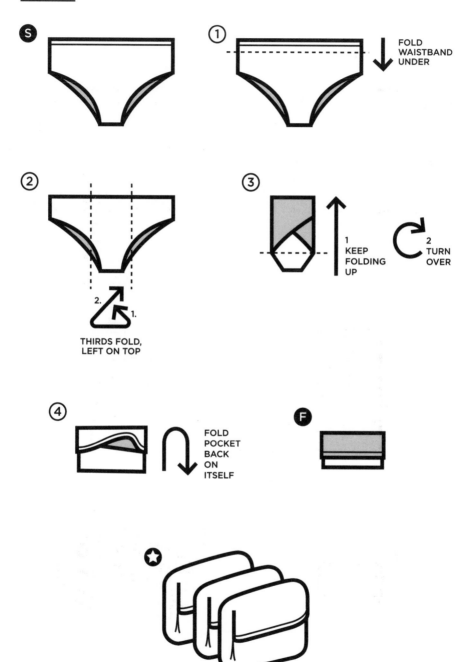

S

1 FOLD WAISTBAND UNDER

2 THIRDS FOLD, LEFT ON TOP

3 1 KEEP FOLDING UP 2 TURN OVER

4 FOLD POCKET BACK ON ITSELF

F

★

THONGS

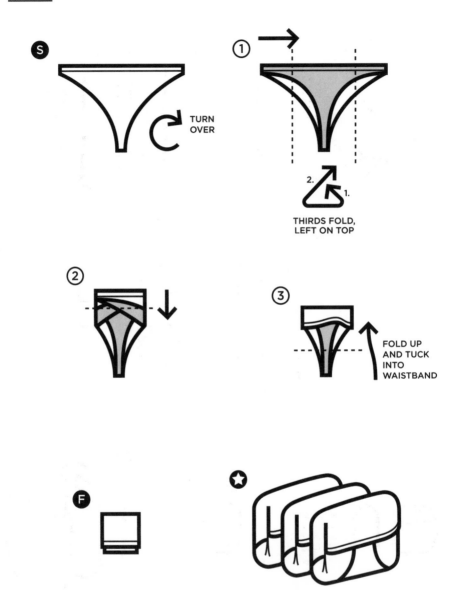

S

TURN
OVER

1

THIRDS FOLD,
LEFT ON TOP

2. 1.

2

3

FOLD UP
AND TUCK
INTO
WAISTBAND

F

SOCKS

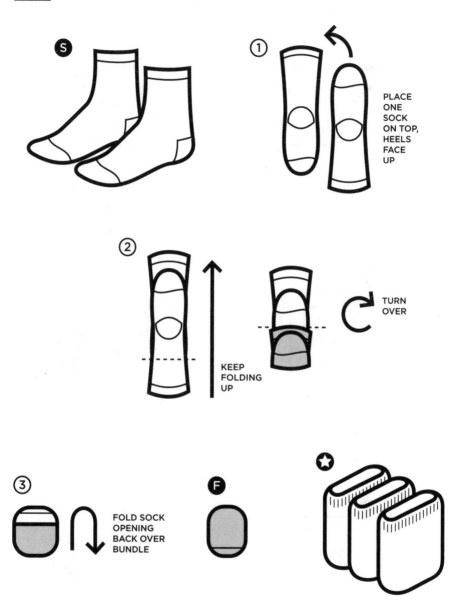

S

① PLACE ONE SOCK ON TOP, HEELS FACE UP

② KEEP FOLDING UP

TURN OVER

③ FOLD SOCK OPENING BACK OVER BUNDLE

F

TRAINER SOCKS

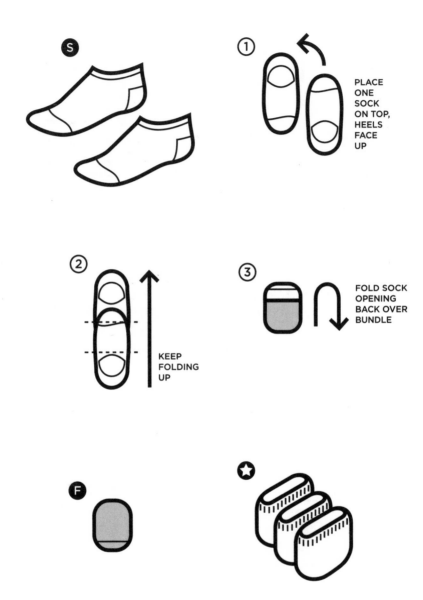

S

① PLACE ONE SOCK ON TOP, HEELS FACE UP

② KEEP FOLDING UP

③ FOLD SOCK OPENING BACK OVER BUNDLE

F

NO-SHOW SOCKS

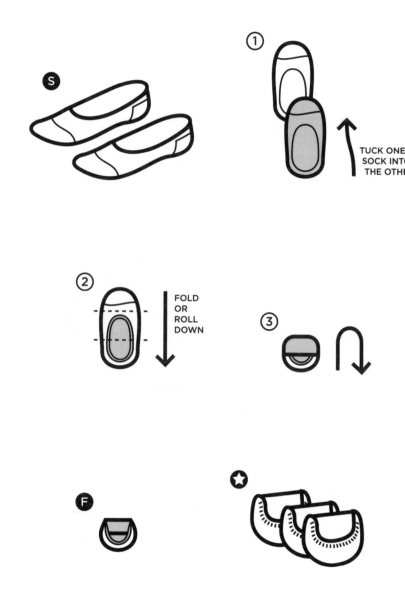

S

① TUCK ONE SOCK INTO THE OTHER

② FOLD OR ROLL DOWN

③

F

★

WARDROBE

Your wardrobe should be used as easy access to all your everyday pieces, as well as storage for clothes you don't want to fold.

A casual wardrobe of everyday items makes your morning that bit smoother. You can just get up and go grab your outfit. And this may mean there's a mixture of jeans, coats, dresses and more in there, but the After Value of having these everyday items together will save you time not only in selection but also putting away, as these are the clothes being washed the most and therefore put away the most. (Note that your everyday casual wardrobe can change over time as you replace old with new and the seasons change so you swap out items for more weather-appropriate or new clothing.)

I also use this space to hang things I'm trying to wear more because I know that if they're with my everyday clothes, I see them often and they're easy to access so I am more likely to wear them. Organise hanging clothes by colour for an attractive display and calmer feel.

A tip I love to share is when you purchase something new, hang it in your everyday casual wardrobe (and don't put it away somewhere 'for special'). By seeing it more frequently you will naturally assess your need for it, and if it's not worn within the returns period you are much more likely to return it and release that space back to the room – and prevent money being wasted. Impulse purchases are all too common and I have found things in the drawer with labels on a year later. We need to make this change for our bank balance, for the environment and for our homes.

HANGING HACKS

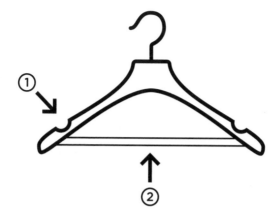

1   Grooves on hangers are useful for clothes with clothing straps. These straps prevent the clothing from slipping off the hanger and also take some weight off, easing pressure from the seems of the clothes.

2   The bar gives you the extra option of hanging trousers, long dresses or cardigans.

When it comes to hanging your items, the biggest piece of life-changing advice I can give you is to invest in a set of decent hangers. Using the same hangers throughout will save a lot of space and keep the space tidy and looking great. The type of hanger is really up to you and your needs/preferences. I would expect that the thinner the hanger, the more clothes you will fit in, but one follower told me they use the thick wooden ones as they take up more space, preventing them buying more clothes... Life hack right there!

Extendable rails are also useful to create extra hanging space in an area. They are easy to fit, with just three screws on each side. You might remember seeing that in The Flat I had double-hanging space and I kept tops on the high rail and trousers and jeans on the low rail.

ALTERNATIVE JEANS HANGING FOLD

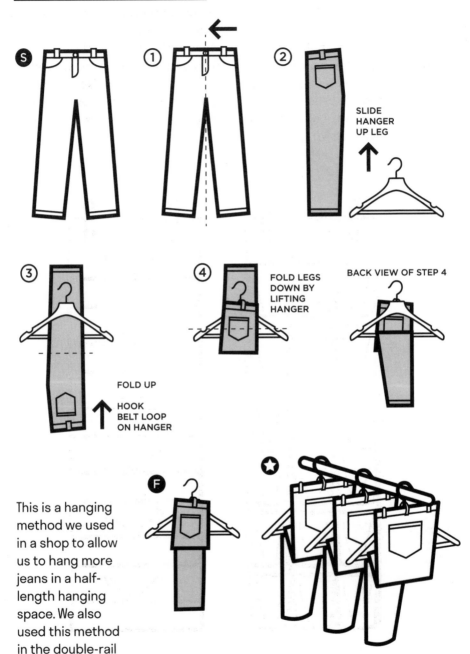

S

1

2 SLIDE HANGER UP LEG

3 FOLD UP

HOOK BELT LOOP ON HANGER

4 FOLD LEGS DOWN BY LIFTING HANGER

BACK VIEW OF STEP 4

F

This is a hanging method we used in a shop to allow us to hang more jeans in a half-length hanging space. We also used this method in the double-rail wardrobe in The Flat.

WARDROBE SPACE-SAVING PRODUCTS

My favourite wardrobe organisers are hanging shelves, such as the SKUBB range in IKEA. These can be used for shoes but also smaller items, such as tops, bras, ties and gymwear. They can be hung on the rail or on the back of the wardrobe door and they save so much space (and can be somewhere to put those awkward-to-hang items, like off-the-shoulder tops, or bras, if you want to get them out of the drawers and keep them organised). By adding hanging shelves you add a whole new section to your wardrobe.

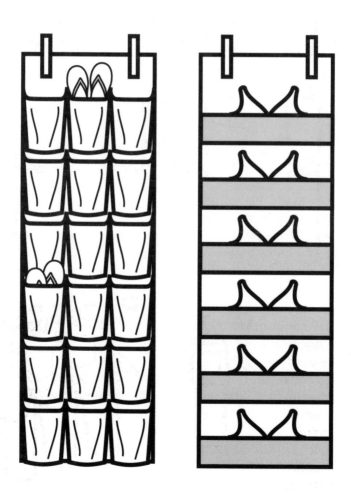

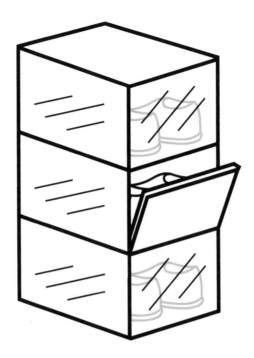

I have two recommendations for keeping shoes in order: the first is an extendable shoe rack which you can keep in the bottom of your wardrobe; the second is shoe boxes (but make sure you buy those that are stackable and that open at the front rather than the top). Ideally, these should be clear boxes so you can see what is inside, making it less likely that shoes get forgotten and remain unworn. And boxes are a particularly good idea if your footwear gets a bit smelly.

If you do find you've not worn some shoes in a while, ask yourself if it's time to donate them. Shoes can take up a lot of space and cause wardrobe frustrations so keep them to a minimum.

SIDE NOTE ON SHOES

There is one more place in your home where you need to create shoe storage and that, of course, is in your entrance or hall. I recommend a shoe cabinet or rack, but the key to successful shoe storage as you enter the home is that whatever shoes live here must only be those being worn throughout the week. Any extras must go away in the bedroom or wardrobe.

An entrance RESET may be necessary to evaluate what you are storing in this area and to communicate this rule to the house and get everyone making a conscious effort to put shoes away. An overspill of shoes in the hallway is such a cause of bad energy. When you walk in from work or school, the first thing you want to see is a calm space and to be able to easily put your bag down and kick off your shoes. What you don't want to do is come home and trip over footwear! Have an entrance that welcomes you home calmly, whatever type of day you've had.

BEDSIDE TABLE

Moving away from clothing storage, I find bedside tables are a funny size so my recommendation is to keep these for little essentials like skincare, books and chargers. If organised thoughtfully, once you're in bed you will have no reason to have to get out! How great does that sound! Because of the size this is a perfect opportunity to use your small-drawer storage ideas, if you have a drawer, to give everything a compartment.

The top/main drawer should be skincare for your night-time skincare routine. Keeping it next to your bed means you're more likely to keep the routine up.

And a book. Whether you avidly read or not, you should always have a book on your bedside table. I am a big believer in books, especially for when watching TV in bed doesn't appeal. Even if you read one page. And if it's a good book, you will never just read one page. . .

Other ideas for things to keep in your bedside table are:

- Make-up/skincare
- Electronics, such as a mobile phone and charger. (For your wires, google 'wire organiser'. You can buy tiny little wire holders that stick to your bedside table or a desk and hold the end of the charger in place so you'll never lose it down the side of your bed again!)
- Diary, note pad or pens for brain dumps before bed
- For new parents – nappies, wipes, creams, changing clothes

UNDERBED STORAGE

This area is easy to forget about, or not make good use of. Here are a few thoughts:

- Do choose storage containers with lids or zippable seals (it can get very dusty under your bed) to keep items contained and together
- Do store items under there that you don't need to access as often; for example, bedding, extra jumpers, towels and holiday clothes
- Do buy drawers on wheels that will create functional storage under beds that lasts. Often underbed drawers are sold separately so it's worth checking back with the shop you bought your bed from to see if there are any matching options
- Don't use this space to store anything you use daily

BEDDING

For me, changing the bed used to be such a laborious task. Now, not so much. I still don't love doing it but, as with all housework, it has to be done so I've made it easier for myself. I figured out that the reason it seemed to take so long was that I spent most of the time looking for matching bedding, and while I was looking for matching bedding I would end up ruining all the folded piles in the cupboard, so then I'd have to tidy that up!

The first thing I thought about was: 'If I can only have one set of bedding on my bed at a time, why the hell do I own 20?' They took up a whole cupboard! This was space that could be used for other things, or just space that could be clear with nothing to tidy up. So I considered the minimum amount of bedding I could use, and here's my conclusion:

1. A set on the bed
2. A set in the wash
3. A spare set just in case you need an emergency changeover

So three sets! That's how many bedding sets are in my house per bed – max. (I also have Christmas bedding but that goes in the loft for 11 months of the year). You might want extra sets for babies/young children and fewer for the spare room too. This has freed up so much space in the airing cupboard and I spend no time at all looking for bedding now. (Plus it's helped me to get rid of old bedding that was past its best but that I held on to 'just in case'.)

My priority here is not to save space – that is just a bonus. The priority is to encourage me to regularly change the bed by making it a seamless task.

Now let's look at the crucial household linen folds which are going to make for a satisfying airing cupboard.

BEDDING FOLDS

I use the same fold for all sizes of bedding, this way I can remember it well and the airing cupboard looks uniform. The only difference is that the larger-size bedding results in a larger end product. So here is my main bedding-folding technique. With duvets, bedspreads, or comforters, you can also use the ranger roll or fold.

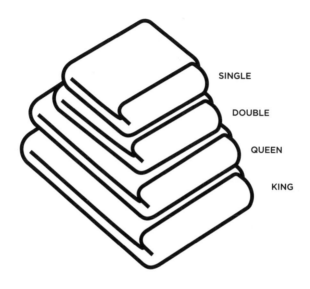

SINGLE

DOUBLE

QUEEN

KING

TIP
Store your bedding in sets: sheets,
pillow-cases and covers kept together (perhaps
within a pillow-case from the set).

FITTED SHEET FOLD

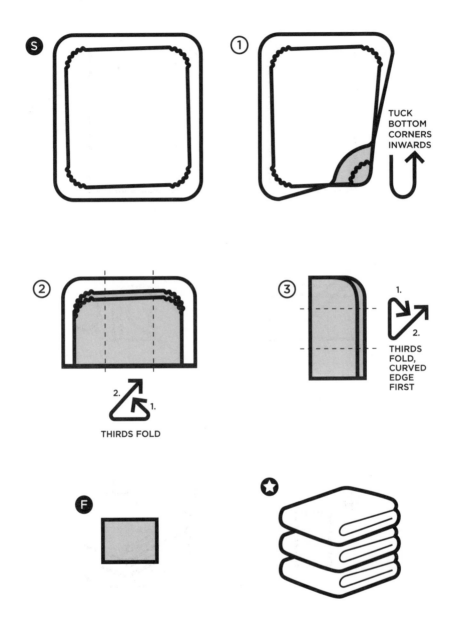

PILLOW-CASE FOLD

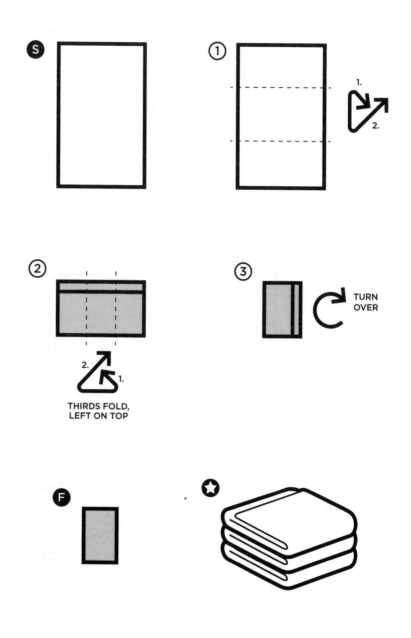

DUVET FOLD

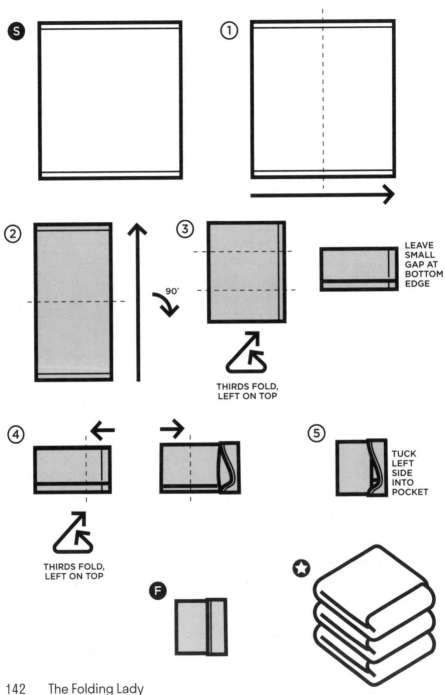

S

1

2

90°

3

LEAVE SMALL GAP AT BOTTOM EDGE

THIRDS FOLD, LEFT ON TOP

4

THIRDS FOLD, LEFT ON TOP

5

TUCK LEFT SIDE INTO POCKET

F

★

CHILDREN'S BEDROOMS

I am a massive fan of all children's rooms being organised, clear and calm spaces – yes, that might sound crazy! One of the big things I took away from my Early Childhood Studies degree is how important environment is in relation to a child's behaviour. Everything counts – the colour, the furniture, the textures... This sounds really over the top, but it's about making some simple choices. These choices will help their room to be a calming, educational space that promotes choice, independence and better sleep. The great thing about making these choices is that, as a parent, they will make your life easier too. I promise!

TOYS

Toy mess is a constant with small children. It is something you must make peace with because the foundations of children's learning are in play, and so the opportunity to play is important, especially in a child's early years. (But I also believe play is so important throughout life.) Skills such as language, problem solving, social and emotional development – to name just a few – are developed through play. And of course, this is not just about toys, but also the space and environment you have for play.

As we let the play take place for our children's learning and development, it is inevitable that some mess is created. The important thing is that it is quick and easy to tidy up. If you are someone who has a dedicated room for toys, then there are so many ways in which that room could be set up to get the most out of the space for your child, but let's assume we have a bedroom or a small area in the home where all the toys are kept and play takes place.

To be able to tidy up quickly, my best recommendation is simple storage bins or boxes which toys can be simply thrown into at night. If these bins are in an open space, choose ones with lids so that the toys are not seen or accessible to the child past bedtime (for the adults' benefit also). Preferably, toys would be kept in a closed space.

When we first started lockdown, we were in the flat and didn't have a lot of space. There was also worry about money as I had been put on furlough so I didn't want Arthur to get bored with his toys. I separated his toys and put half of them in the loft. After six weeks we gathered a few toys from the bedroom he wasn't playing with and swapped them out for some in the loft. It was like he'd been given brand new toys and this stopped our home being overwhelmed.

TIP
Every year, in October, I do a big toy sort and purge.
I choose October as we are near to Christmas and
it will create space for new toys and games.

I'm also a big believer in toys going away at bedtime so us adults have some time where we don't have to look at them everywhere! Here are some storage ideas that look like trendy furniture but double up as secret toy storage and can be used in any room:

- ▶ **Ottomans** – we had a lovely teal one in our living room at The Flat. It looked like part of the furniture and also doubled up as extra seating when we had guests. It was so easy to throw the toys into it at the end of the day.

- ▶ **Cube storage units** – these are great because you can organise your toys by category in each cube. Choose cubes that match your décor, so no one will know they are full of toys.

- ▶ **Storage baskets** – not small ones, more laundry bin in size. For George, I used them for his dressing-up clothes which can be bulky, so this is a great space-saver for the wardrobe. Storage baskets are also quick to throw things into for a quick tidy-up.

BOOK CORNER

A book corner is a great space to encourage reading and calm time. Shelves at child height on the wall with front-facing books allow younger children to select their own books and see all their choices. Picture-ledge shelves like the IKEA MOSSLANDA ones are perfect for this type of display.

Bring the area together with a comfy beanbag or some big floor cushions for a lovely book space. Putting the books away on these shelves is also an easy job as it doesn't require any sort of order. It looks good however the books are put back, so it's a tidying activity for children that promotes ownership of their space from a very young age.

SECRET SPACE

Children really benefit from a little 'secret space' such as a tent – an area that makes them feel like no one can see them. Here they can calm down if needed, take time out from other people, and play alone, which is a very natural way to play for smaller children. The After Value you get from giving your child a secret space is sky high, not just for us parents but the child as well.

> **Keeping as much as you can at child height gives them more opportunity to be independent at tidying up and catering to their own play needs.**

For parents, this can also double up as a quick toy-tidy storage area where you can throw all the toys at the end of day. We have Arthur's secret space (a simple pop-up tent from IKEA) in the living room as his bedroom is too small for it, but he loves it and so do all the other kids when they visit. This tent can quickly be put up and taken down, so it's perfect if you don't have a large space to house certain things permanently. For this in particular you really don't need much space – a corner will do.

CLOTHES

If you are trying to save space in your child's bedroom, I would recommend using drawers only, because most children's clothes can be folded easily. If space is something you have plenty of, then wardrobes are practical storage for clothes, dress-up items and bulky things that may take up a lot of space in the drawers (but still can be folded down if a wardrobe is not available). Again, everything can be folded.

For baby and toddler clothes start with the drawer boxes and as they grow you will naturally move on to extendable drawer dividers. For example, the boxes are handy when they are little because they are transportable, so you can take a set of baby grows to another part of the house with you in the daytime, use as you need and then simply put them back into the drawer at bedtime. No fuss, no mess, no effort!

"

When putting laundry away, make the effort to turn items the right way round. Morning routines with kids can be rowdy and stressful and sometimes the last thing you want when you've got your young child to the point of dressing is to have to turn their clothes the right way round.

"

BABY CLOTHES

BABY GROW FOLD

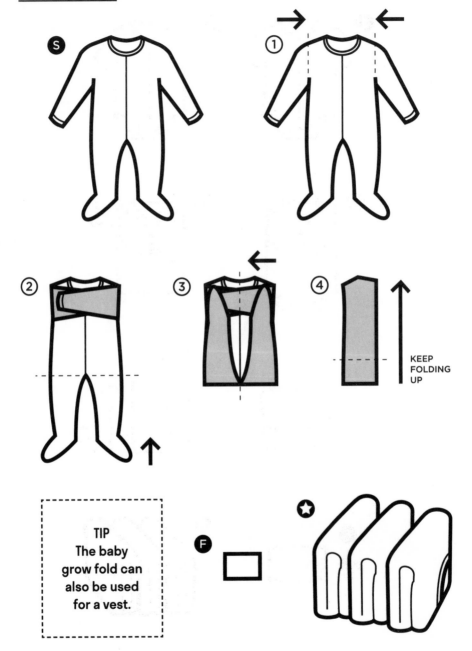

KEEP
FOLDING
UP

TIP
The baby
grow fold can
also be used
for a vest.

BABY VEST FOLD

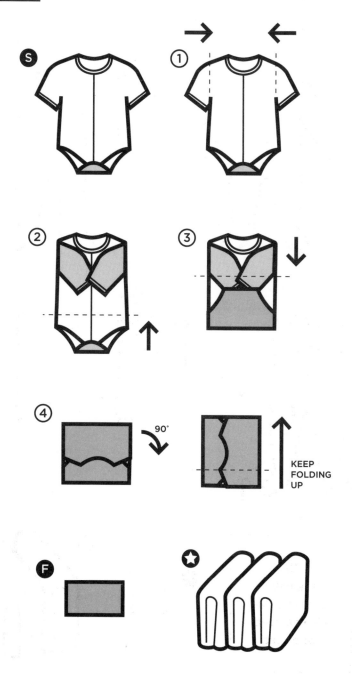

BABY ACCESSORIES

There are many options for folding blankets and muslin cloths, because they are a simple rectangle shape. I will show you two options here (and you can also use the folds for bedding and towels, see pages 141–142 and 185–187). These two folds work particularly well for shelves and drawers.

BABY BLANKET/MUSLIN FOLD 1

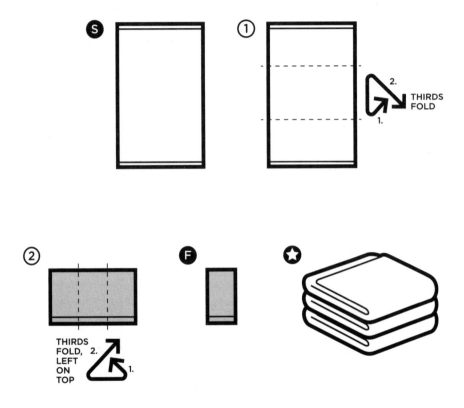

BABY BLANKET/MUSLIN FOLD 2

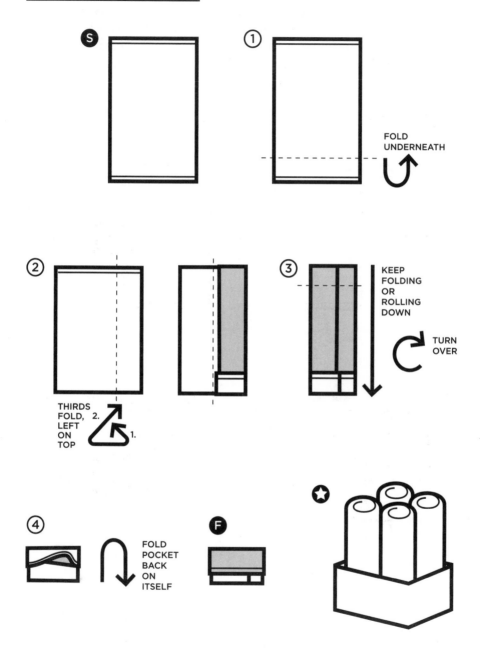

S

① FOLD UNDERNEATH

② THIRDS FOLD, LEFT ON TOP 2. 1.

③ KEEP FOLDING OR ROLLING DOWN

TURN OVER

④ FOLD POCKET BACK ON ITSELF

F

CLOTHES FOR TODDLERS AND OLDER CHILDREN

As Arthur has grown I still use the box containers in drawers, but for some items I'll be moving to extendable drawer dividers very soon. For now, I use all size boxes as he has a bed with built-in drawers that are deep so I can fit lots in them. The lovely thing about having the clothes in drawers as the children get older is that they can become independent and choose their own outfits. I find most wardrobes are usually too high up for young children to reach their clothes.

LEGGINGS/JOGGERS FOLD

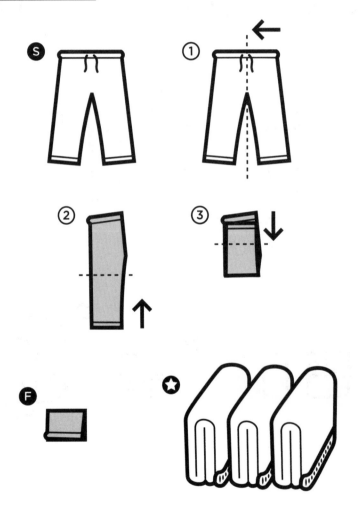

TIGHTS FOLD

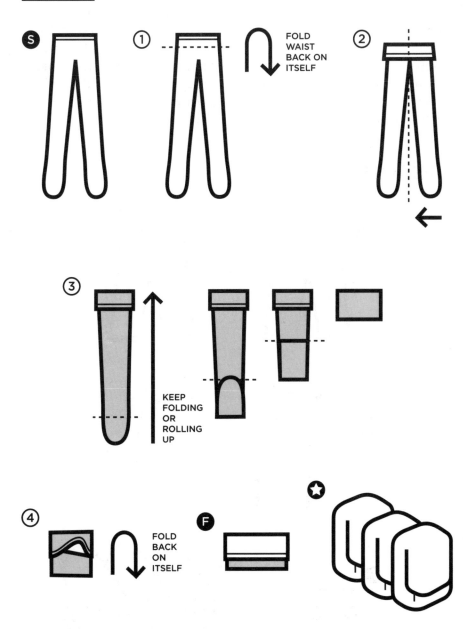

S

① FOLD WAIST BACK ON ITSELF

②

③ KEEP FOLDING OR ROLLING UP

④ FOLD BACK ON ITSELF

F

★

T-SHIRTS AND TOPS FOLD FOR DRAWER

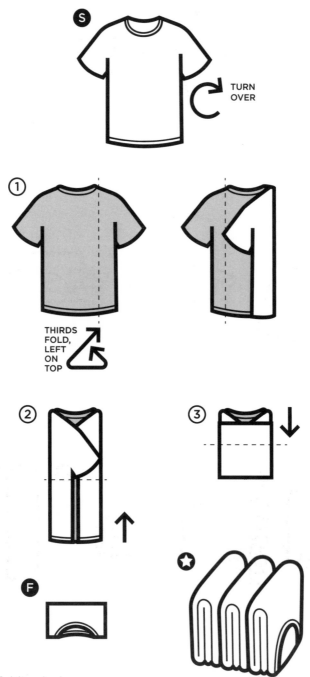

DRESSES FOLD FOR DRAWER

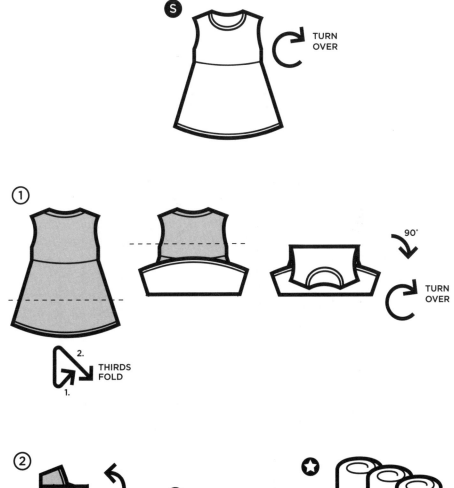

S TURN OVER

1 90° TURN OVER

2. THIRDS FOLD
1.

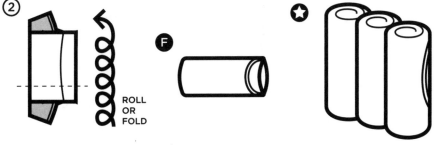

2 ROLL OR FOLD

F

★

PYJAMAS FOLD FOR DRAWER

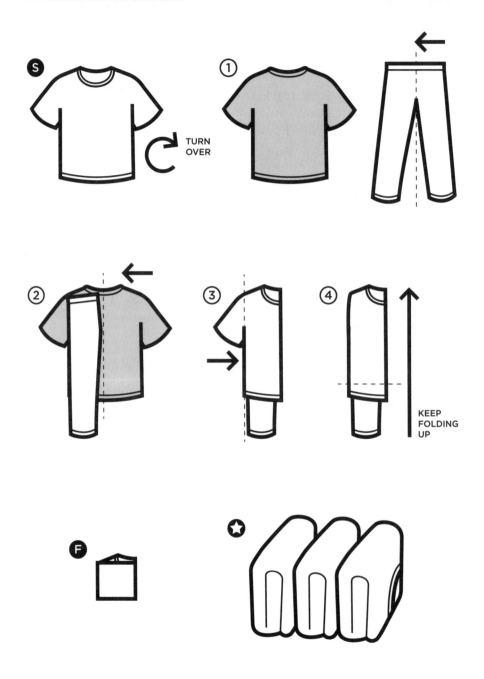

TURN OVER

KEEP FOLDING UP

IMPORTANT POINTS FOR THE BEDROOM

► Keep this room tidy and as clear as possible so you can wake up and sleep in a calm and orderly space.

► Create a capsule wardrobe of clothes you wear often.

► Don't pack drawers too tight to avoid deep creases.

► Ensure clothes for a shelf are folded flat, flat, flat!

► Store your most-worn items in the most accessible place, i.e. the front of the drawer rather than the back.

My favourite products for the bedroom are:

- Drawer dividers
- Wardrobe hanging storage
- Hangers

My favourite folds for the bedroom are:

- Socks fold
- Boxers fold
- Kids' pyjamas fold

LET'S TALK ABOUT THE LAUNDRY

I always get asked how I keep on top of my laundry. When I think about it, I do have some rituals and routines that really work for me and could help you. Before I get into them, I want to ask you to get rid of your negative thinking about laundry. This comes first. You need to make peace with the fact that laundry is never done. There, I said it!

And you might not like it right now but it's true. As long as we continue to wear clothes, there will always be laundry. So why spend your time moaning and feeling down about a job that's not going away? You'll drive yourself crazy with this mindset. Instead, put the task into your daily routine and make time for it, and also look to improve the laundry environment – make sure you've got the washing tablets/detergent stored near by and you aren't needing to constantly move objects to get to the machine. If what you are doing isn't working for you, then try something else because if you continue in the same way you can only expect the same results.

Here are some laundry truths from my house that work for me. I don't love doing laundry, but I also don't hate it; and it's always going to be there so I don't believe in wasting energy being annoyed by it.

> ► We do not use a laundry basket – when we lived in The Flat and were trying to make more room, ready for Arthur's arrival, I realised that my laundry basket was taking up a whole cupboard. When I really considered it, I was just using it as another space to put clothes so I didn't have to put them away. I needed that space more, so I chucked the basket away. From then on, I put a wash on, put it out to dry and then when it was dry put it away immediately. This got me into a sound routine of putting clothes away quicker but also being mindful of putting a wash on and finding the time to tidy it away on the same day.

- Put your clothes away straight from the dryer or the rack – this is also the best time to put them away as there should be the fewest creases at this point. More so if they've just come out of the dryer.

- Get rid of laundry bags in the bedroom. If you don't see it, you stop talking about it. And you stop doing it. We have ours in the hallway, or kitchen when I carry it down.

- Put a wash on every day – little and often always wins and this is a realistic way to get it into your routine. I keep my routine weekly. If I am too specific and assign certain days to tasks, then there is more to fall behind on. I'm not much of a forward planner so if I know what I need to do in the week I can plan it around events rather than plan the events round the house. Having said that, I know many have certain days for sports kit, bedding changes or towel washes.

- Use the timer – when I used to work at the store I would put a wash on at night and time it to come on and be finished by the time I woke up. This is revolutionary! Then I would put it on the drying racks before work and it would be ready to put away when I got home. It also meant that I didn't have to constantly look at washing as it was only out when I was out of the house.

KITCHEN

This space for me is so much fun to organise but such a massive job!

The main aims of your kitchen space are that that it enables you to cook, clean, eat and socialise with ease. These actions cover our basic needs and any kitchen requirements on top of that will be personal to you. Your kitchen should be so easy to navigate that you will be motivated to cook even if it's not your thing. You want to be able to decide to bake a cake and then go straight to your kitchen and start that action: no clearing a space first, no 20-minute searching aimlessly for ingredients in different places, no time wasted locating the cookbook. And during and at the end of the action everything should be easy to clear away. Plus a well-organised kitchen that's set up to suit your current lifestyle is super-quick and a joy to tidy up!

The kitchen is also often a family hub and a communal area used by everyone for many different reasons, so recognising the wants and needs of the space should be relatively easy as lots of daily interaction and communication take place here. Engage the others that use it and gather ideas so you understand what will work for everyone. Observe how people use the space differently and your planning will be much more meaningful, better received and more likely to provide great After Value.

There are so many different areas to consider – the fridge, pantry, cleaning items, cutlery, utensils, cookware, crockery. . . and always plenty of miscellaneous extras. Because of this there are many RESETs that may be needed. If you feel overwhelmed, remember to break the spaces down. You don't need to do everything at once.

WHAT WORKS IN OUR KITCHEN

Everyone's requirements and preferences will be different. Perhaps your kitchen space works well for you, or perhaps there are areas for improvement. We spend a lot of time in our kitchens each day, so take the necessary time to plan any kitchen-area changes using the RESET process.

Here are some ideas from our home:

OUR NEEDS	HOW WE MAKE IT WORK
I like to blow-dry my hair while sat at the island.	All of my hair bits – hair dryer, straightener, serums have their own drawer in the kitchen.
George takes a packed lunch to school.	In the fridge we have a fridge organiser with a handle with all I need to make his sandwiches in it. Every morning I can just whip it out and get on with making his packed lunch.
Jacob likes to keep the keys in the kitchen. (Yes, we are Shelley and Dan!)	We worked together to find the best solution by running through the RESET plan.
I want to improve my baking skills.	I have a shelf in the corner of the kitchen with all my baking ingredients so I can bake with ease and see what I need from the shops.
George loves a hot chocolate every night before bed.	He has his own hot chocolate drawer with all his flavours and the utensils he needs to make it himself.

THE SUPERMARKET IS YOUR STOCKROOM

If you are short on space or want to keep things minimalistic, think about your shopping methods. Often supermarkets are full of multi-buy offers or bulk-buy options that save us a little bit of money and make us think we've won against them. More often than not though, the After Value of using these offers or bulk-buys is very low, if you do not have the space to store the extra bulk.

Assign your regular foods a boundary (like we spoke about for the clothes) and then make a pact to only shop for that space. The hardest part about stocking up on food is needing to find more than one space for it to go in: one space that you cook from and then another to store the over-stock. If this is not possible, buy storage jars or baskets that are the correct size for a week's worth of that food (or however frequently you shop) and when you shop for more buy a size that will fit the gap you now have.

Now, let's look at some areas of focus that will help create a really great kitchen space for everyone and then you can add your own personal touches. Let's start with the countertops...

COUNTERTOPS

Your countertops are on show and make things easily accessible so they can be great practical surfaces for housing the things you use the most, and you can have fun making them aesthetically pleasing too. Now I understand there are some of you who like the clear-countertops look because you don't like 'clutter' but what if I told you your countertops can make you eat better, encourage you to cook more, and make you unconsciously live the life you want to lead (as much as you can from the kitchen)?

Countertops are what I call an open space – space where everything can be constantly seen. And because everything can be seen, the things you have on display should be encouraging, positive, motivating and/or make you happy. For example, if you wanted to eat healthier foods, you wouldn't put a biscuit tin on your countertop, you'd put out a fruit bowl. And to go further, if you wanted your family to try new fruits, you'd fill the bowl with those fruits and put it centre stage in an open space that everyone was able to access freely.

Here are some other examples of how to use all spaces around the home to inspire lifestyle changes:

I WANT TO...	ACTION TAKEN
...cook more.	Encourage this by putting your cookbooks on an accessible shelf instead of in a cupboard.
...think more positively about myself.	Fill a picture frame with a positive affirmation and hang it next to your coat hook so you see it every time you leave the house.
...exercise more.	Leave your exercise mat in an open space where you will see it every day. The more accessible it is, the more likely you are to exercise.

To encourage a calm, social and personal space, I encourage you to get rid of all food packaging on your fruit, cereals or similar. This could mean emptying food out into containers or putting them in a cupboard. But ultimately – no branding is allowed on your countertops.

In our homes we should free our minds from marketing and subliminal messages. The less marketing and branding, the less distraction. If you need the packet instructions for something, then think about storing that item in a cupboard or keeping the instructions in a folder. Keep labelling to a minimum and only where necessary for organisational benefits, such as herbs and spices. Be in control of what your countertops encourage you to do rather than leaving it to a company's marketing department to guide you.

FRIDGE

I have one main rule for the fridge – contain, contain, CONTAIN!

Putting everything into a fridge organiser will keep your fridge nice and tidy, even when it's at the point of needing a RESET. An organiser will also cut down on your cleaning time as any spillages are restricted and you can pop the container in the dishwasher if needed.

I recommend buying fridge containers/bins that work with the whole depth of your shelves – this way you stay away from creating a front and back section to your fridge (where the back section will never get used as it's hard to get to and hidden away). Create areas in your fridge that match your present lifestyle. For example, I make George sandwiches for school every day so I have a container with a handle that stores all the sandwich stuff. In the morning I come to the fridge, pick the container up and take it to the counter. There is no looking for meat or marg – who's got time for that?! It's all in one place. Let's make life easier on ourselves, yeah! Seamless mornings are so key to the rest of your day. Other people may need designated fridge spaces for medication, baby bits, special foods and so on. What do you want in your fridge? What can you never find in there? Have a real think about it before you start.

The same rule applies to the fridge as the countertops. Get things out that you want to eat more of – so, fruit and veg that need to be in the fridge should be out of their packets and easily accessible. The more accessible they are, the more you'll use them.

▶   Lazy Susans are a great piece of kit to keep your condiments tidy.

▶   Use containers with handles for products you want to take out and use elsewhere in your kitchen.

▶   Take fruit and veg out of their packets so they're easily accessible, encouraging usage.

FOOD PREP AREA

Have one clear space in your kitchen for preparing food. I have a chopping board out in this space to make sure it stays free. It is important that if you want to start cooking or baking, you don't need to start clearing up first. You want to be able to make the decision to cook and have the space ready to immediately start that action. Your most accessible spaces should be kept for the items you use the most. For example, if you enjoy a cup of tea, it would be sensible to have your kettle ready on your countertop rather than in a cupboard, or the toaster or breadmaker if you use them daily.

Okay, how about some folding now?

TEA TOWEL/TABLECLOTH FOLD

Hanging your tea towel on your oven rail is a simple 'Thirds Fold' then hang (see page 186 for towel folding). To fold your rectangular tablecloths, I recommend a 'Thirds and Thirds Again' fold (see page 150 Baby Blanket Fold). To store them in your drawer you can use the following fold:

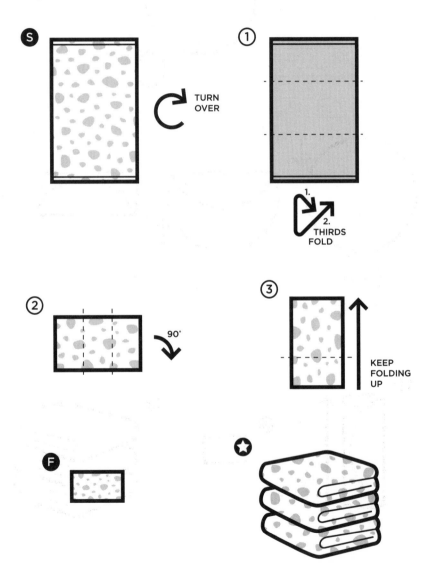

ROUND TABLECLOTH FOLD

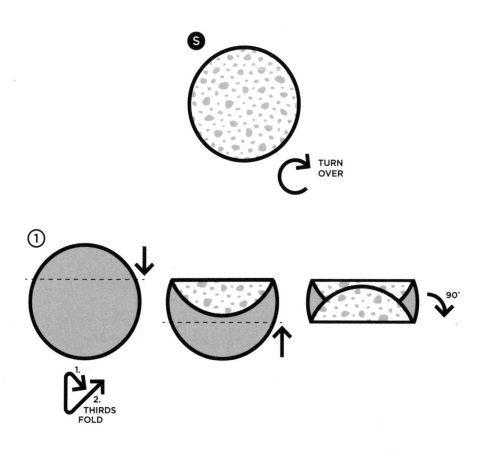

S

TURN OVER

① 1. 2. THIRDS FOLD

90°

② KEEP FOLDING UP

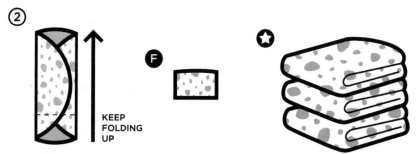

F

APRON FOLD

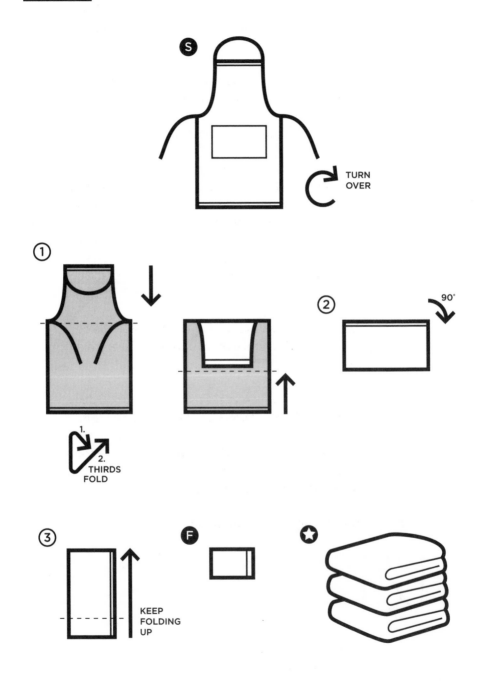

S

TURN OVER

① THIRDS FOLD
1.
2.

② 90°

③ KEEP FOLDING UP

F

★

PANTRY

It is my dream to have a pantry... it is organisation heaven! So many clean lines to be made to look lovely and organised. Here are some of my favourite tips:

▶ Have all the things you want to access most regularly on the middle shelves to save yourself reaching or bending.

▶ Store less-used items higher up.

▶ If the top shelves are too high for you to reach, buy a little step that stays in the pantry at all times to allow you access when you want. Often we put these things in places we can't reach with no access and then they don't get used. We don't want anything taking up space in our homes that doesn't get used. If you find even with access you're not using it, then have a think about if it's really needed.

▶ Use baskets to store individual items such as cereal bars or packets. And store them upright so everything can be seen.

▶ For cans I recommend tiered shelves so you can see every single can. If you can see it, you will use it.

▶ Turntables can be used in corners and for random packets to ensure everything is kept together, accessible and looks great.

▶ Contain and label everything!

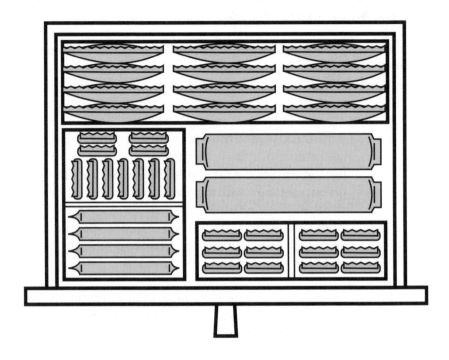

My snack drawer has been an extremely popular feature on my social pages, and also rather controversial because it can seem like an unnecessary thing to have. I get it – arranging your snacks neatly only for them to be eaten in a matter of days. . . But there is some real After Value I get from organising my snack drawer, so it's right for me.

Packed-lunch prep was always a hindrance for me in the mornings, with very little time to wake up and be out of the door to get George to breakfast club and me to work. This is why a lot of the organising I do is to shave seconds off my morning routine; time is precious in the morning and good moods are paramount. (I did try making it in the evenings but working six days a week meant I just wanted to sit down when I got home.) I get in a real bad mood if I can't put a packed lunch together easily – and this wasn't always about the time it took putting it together but more about whether I had the items. I never seemed to notice when we ran out of things and some mornings would have nothing to offer. So I created the 'packed-lunch cupboard', which then evolved to the snack drawer. It was an area I could store all of the snack options for George to take in his packed lunch or to football.

I put some baskets in a drawer and started standing up all the snacks in order. The biscuits had their own space as well as George's favourite breadsticks. I get After Value from organising my snack drawer because:

- ▶ It makes me more aware of when we're low and am more motivated to go to the shops.

- ▶ George can access his snacks with ease so will choose his own and help with the packed lunch.

- ▶ It's made me more aware of which snacks George eats and which he doesn't, so I've stopped wasting my money on things that won't get eaten.

- ▶ I enjoy the organisational satisfaction of putting the snacks way and seeing what it looks like afterwards... A calm drawer of delicious snacks.

- ▶ Everything gets eaten because of the points above – no waste.

DINING TABLE

This is an exciting topic for me! For years, we lacked a proper dining-room table and now we have a fabulous one and I'm obsessed. My tablescaping skills are still in development but I have, of course, mastered a few napkin folds. Last Christmas was quite a moment for me when I went viral on TikTok and Instagram by bringing the Christmas Tree napkin to the masses. At this point we were still in The Flat so we didn't even have a table to display these for ourselves. Christmas Day came in lockdown and then the most heartwarming thing happened. One by one, you all started to send me photos of your Christmas dinner set-ups, adorned with the Christmas Tree napkins. It was truly an amazing moment for me and one which I didn't expect at all! So here it is – my Christmas Tree napkin, the fold that perked up Christmas in lockdown 2020.

CHRISTMAS TREE NAPKIN

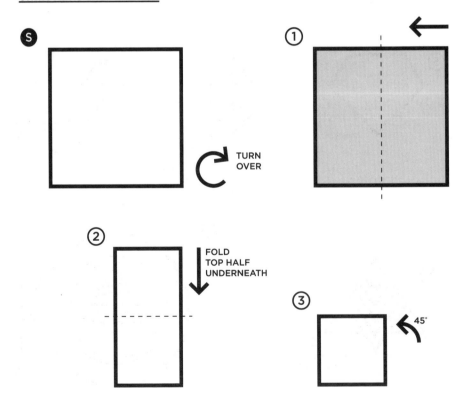

S

① TURN OVER

② FOLD TOP HALF UNDERNEATH

③ 45°

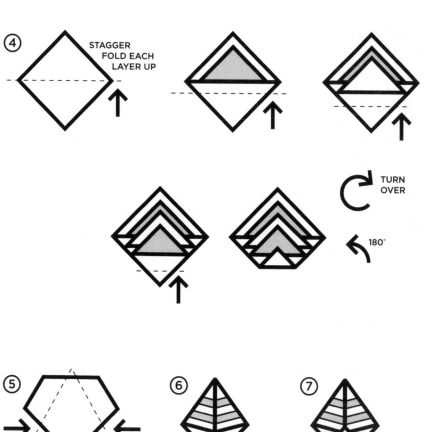

④ STAGGER FOLD EACH LAYER UP

TURN OVER

180°

⑤

⑥

FOLD UP ALL BUT ONE LAYER

⑦

TURN OVER

⑧

FOLD TIPS OF TRIANGLES UNDERNEATH

HALLOWEEN NAPKIN

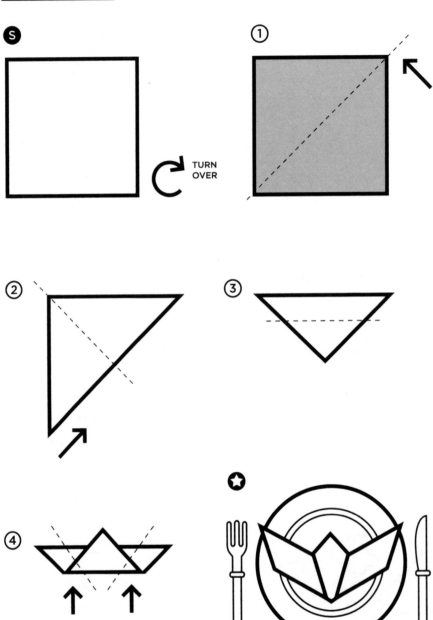

BOW NAPKIN

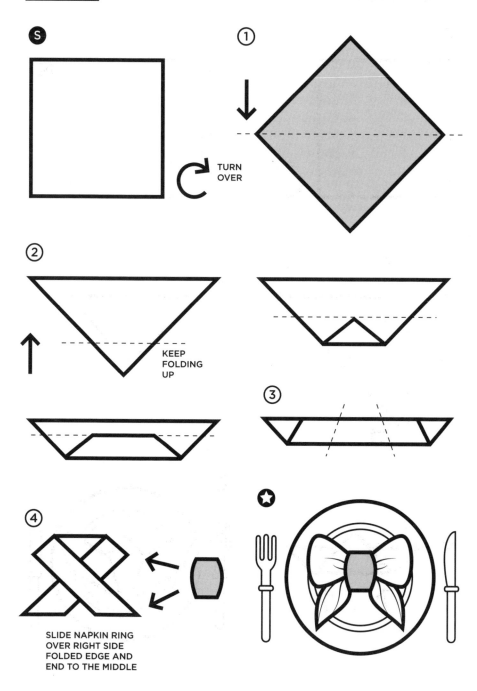

S

1

TURN OVER

2

KEEP FOLDING UP

3

4

SLIDE NAPKIN RING OVER RIGHT SIDE FOLDED EDGE AND END TO THE MIDDLE

IMPORTANT POINTS FOR THE KITCHEN

► Use your countertops as display areas for the things you want to do more.

► The most accessible spaces must house the items you use the most.

► Contain everything in your fridge to avoid mess and spills.

► Remove food packaging where possible to make fruit and veg accessible and to remove marketing from cluttering open spaces.

► Make sure everything in a cupboard can be seen when open. If you can see it you'll use it.

My favourite products for the kitchen are:

· Tiered cupboard shelves
· Lazy Susan (in the fridge or cupboards)
· Glass jars/dishes for storing leftovers in the fridge – better for you and the environment
· Fridge organisers/containers

My favourite fold for the kitchen is:

· Ranger roll for tea towels

"

The main aims of your kitchen space are that that it enables you to cook, clean, eat and socialise with ease. These actions cover our basic needs and any kitchen requirements on top of that will be personal to you.

"

BATHROOM

This section is going to be so much fun! The bathroom is another communal area of the home where you can add some lovely little touches that will create a lot of After Value for you, the rest of the family and anyone that visits.

In this section we're going to talk a lot about towels and flannels but we'll also touch on cosmetics and bath accessories. Organisation is key in the bathroom because you want to keep personal necessities in there which you might not want in view all of the time, or for when guests need to pop in. It needs to be super-functional if it is the space where you get ready each morning.

Just like the kitchen, this is a space that everyone uses but, unlike the kitchen, it's not as social... We don't hang out in the bathroom and chat. If we're in the bathroom it's for a purpose and so it's important that the area is set up to enable us to get in, crack on and get out. Especially if, like us, you have one bathroom between all of you.

Finally, the bathroom is a space that is cleaned often, so to have it organised and clear will encourage you by making this process nice and quick. Can you tell I'm not a fan of cleaning?

BATHROOM FOLDS

I'm going to let you into a secret about my towel folding – and this doesn't just work for the towels but for anything that's a rectangle: bedsheets, tea towels, tablecloths... It's simply the 'Thirds and Thirds Again' fold.

You can fold your towel in half again and again until it's at a manageable size (you won't need to do this so much for towels but will for bedsheets). Quite often we fold really well but the loose edges make it look messy. When used on three or four different sizes of the same towel style, it can make an attractive towel stack which is perfect to put on your guest bed so they have all the fresh towels they need. You can do this for yourself of course too – and then pretend you're staying in a fancy hotel!

TOWEL FOLD

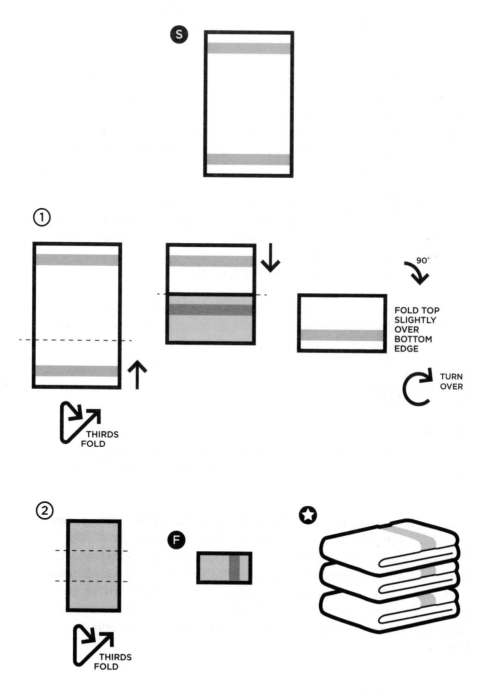

S

1

↑ THIRDS FOLD

↓

90°

FOLD TOP
SLIGHTLY
OVER
BOTTOM
EDGE

TURN
OVER

2

THIRDS
FOLD

F

☆

HAND TOWEL FOLD

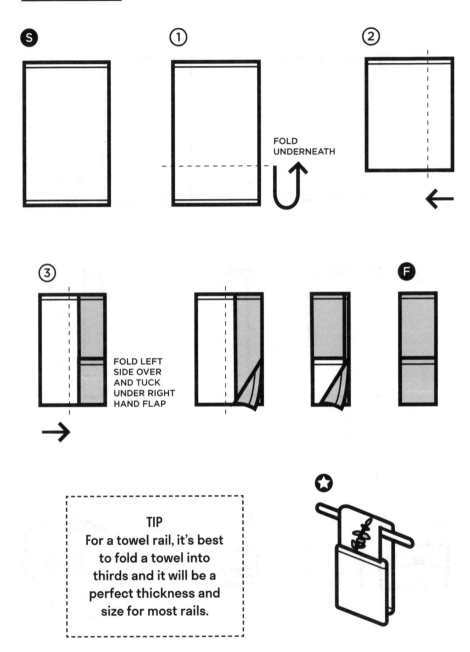

FOLD UNDERNEATH

FOLD LEFT SIDE OVER AND TUCK UNDER RIGHT HAND FLAP

TIP
For a towel rail, it's best to fold a towel into thirds and it will be a perfect thickness and size for most rails.

HAND TOWEL/FLANNEL RANGER ROLL

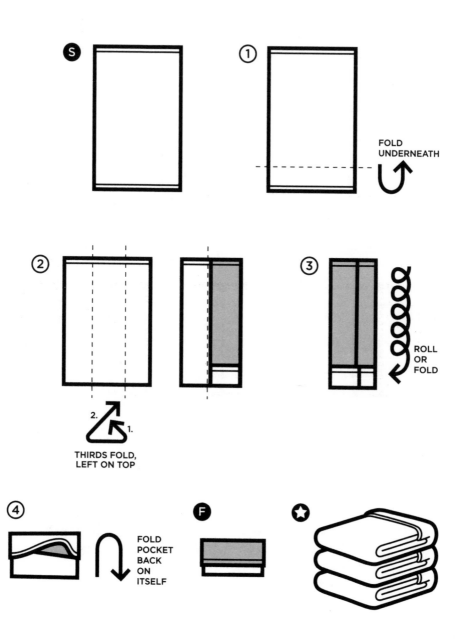

S

1

FOLD
UNDERNEATH

2

THIRDS FOLD,
LEFT ON TOP

3

ROLL
OR
FOLD

4

FOLD
POCKET
BACK
ON
ITSELF

F

BATHROOM COUNTERTOPS

This is where things can get messy! There is something I need you to commit to doing... If something is finished, then take it to the bin and throw it away! You hear me? Most messy bathrooms are made worse with empty bottles of shampoo or soap. There are four easy methods for tidying the lotions, potions and hair care:

1. **Baskets** – a simple waterproof basket will allow you to keep everything together and give easy access to all the soaps when in the bath or shower. You could have a basket per person.

2. **Refillable soap/shampoo dispensers** – these will not only save space but make for a more streamlined and decorative way to display these items. This is also another way of taking brands out of the bathroom – a place you should be able to relax in and not be marketed to. These are widely available in stores and online to suit your taste and budget. You can, of course, buy plain ones online and use a label maker or you can buy labels to suit your décor – I highly recommend visiting The Label Lady on IG for this. She ships worldwide and has a great selection of ready-made or bespoke labels.

3. **Shower storage** – effective shower storage makes such a big change to the look and way you use the bathroom; rustproof, attractive and sturdy is what you need. I am a big fan of Shower Gems as they can be placed on the wall within your shower making everything accessible while showering. They also don't rust and can be taken off without ruining your tiles because of the special glue. Do you remember them from *Dragons' Den*? That is where I first saw them!

4. **Cupboards** – baskets or boxes in your cupboards are a great way to store similar items together or more discreet bathroom items or the products you find get messy quickly.

MAKE-UP AND SKINCARE

I'm adding make-up and skincare to the bathroom but essentially these products need to go wherever you apply your make-up. This could be your bedroom, kitchen or living room. Earlier I recommended keeping your night routine skincare on/in your bedside table. The first question I would ask is: are you a make-up hoarder? If you can answer yes, then let me tell you I once was as well and (unless you're a professional make-up artist) you need to listen up!

If you are not finding the After Value in your make-up collection, you may have too much and it is overwhelming both you and your space. Choose the area where you would like to keep your make-up, and this creates your new make-up boundary. Collect together all of your make-up and lay it out. Now pick out your most frequently worn products and put them in their designated space. Next, choose your proud-to-own products (mine is my Mariah Carey lip gloss from MAC, I hardly every wear it and it's super-old but I love owning it and its packaging is so pretty) and make sure these have their own space. When your drawer is full you should be left with the products you don't use and no longer need. Throw them away if they are past the use-by dates or donate to a friend.

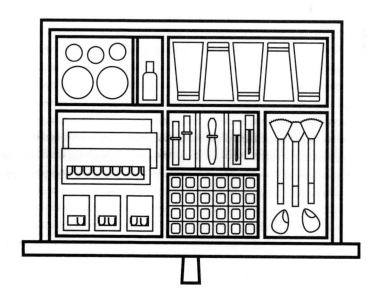

STORAGE WINNERS FOR MAKE-UP

1. **Drawer** – for this mode of storage, use drawer divider trays (and I recommend laying everything flat so you can see what is there easily). Remember: if you see it, you will use it!

   Make sure everything is arranged with your most-used products at the front of your drawer, and that there is an easily accessible section for 'daily routine make-up'. This is for your usuals and by putting this together there's no time wasted on searching. You will also find it is easy to keep the area tidy as you can just throw your most-used items back into one area. If you are working with a deep drawer, use deeper storage bins rather than trays and everything stands vertical, with the label/colouring facing up. The benefit here is that colours of products are usually on the bottom so storing these like this will allow for quick and easy selection.

2. **A transportable make-up bag** – this is my current choice because I like to move around the house to do my make-up. This is mainly because I need to keep watching the baby! It's worth investing in a professional make-up artist's bag if this suits your lifestyle as they are set up for success! My go-to brand is MYKITCO (look on their IG or online beauty stores). My bag was £100 but the After Value is immense. I can do my make-up around where the baby is or even where the best lighting in the house is, successfully. Maybe when Arthur is older and doesn't need supervising, I can go back to having a desk but for now this works well for me.

3. **Display pots** – if you would like some or all of your make-up on display, buy clear plastic drawers and pots which are stackable and will look great on a vanity unit or make-up table. My only issue with these is they get smeared with make-up easily so require good cleaning upkeep, but they are a good option.

IMPORTANT POINTS FOR THE BATHROOM

▶   There is limited storage in a bathroom so think about what you really use the room for to decide what will give you the most After Value in terms of the space.

▶   Remember to use products that are proven not to rust. There is a lot of money spent on storage for a bathroom and your items must be able to live in that steamy environment.

▶   Fold towels into thirds for neater edges, and use fun towel folds to add some frivolity!

My favourite product for the bathroom is:

•   Shower Gem

My favourite folds in the bathroom are:

•   Thirds and Thirds Again
•   Ranger Roll for flannels

PACKING
FOR TRAVEL

Travelling can be one of the most stressful activities imaginable, but as I travel in my older years I have realised it's a great opportunity to sit back and relax because a lot of the time you are sitting down with nothing to do. Who wouldn't want to be told to do that?

In this section, I'm going to show you some really useful ways to pack, and folds that are great for travel. I also include some hints and inspiration on how to make the travel part of any trip as enjoyable as possible with the kids in tow!

PACKING A SUITCASE

The first ingredient in successful travel is a quality suitcase. You need to invest in this as it's something that will last for years and get a huge amount of use, especially if you are a frequent traveller. Quality suitcases come with a selection of helpful compartments/dividers/organisers, good security and some even have chargers or similar built in. The After Value from a good suitcase is immense.

THE FRONT POCKET

This has its own section because I want you to know how important it is, especially with regard to hand luggage. Use this front pocket for things you may need access to during travelling and you'll understand what I mean. It's a vital resource for things you're not putting in your handbag or laptop case – things of secondary importance but that give you plenty of After Value. For example, I like to put face wipes in mine because if I'm travelling for a long time, then running a face wipe over my face will immediately make me feel better. You get the idea? Jacob likes to keep the plug part to a charger in there just in case there are no USB ports available. Think about something that you may not need continual access to but may be needed or helpful at some point.

PACKING CUBES

Next, get some packing cubes. These are available from many online retailers and stores (I bought a set six years ago for £10 and they are still as good as new today). Cubes will help you to divide your belongings up so things are easier to find. They come in a pack with different sizes and shapes; you may not use them all, depending on the size of your case and how long your trip is. Using the cubes allows you to use most of the same folds from the home so you should be able to pack straight from the drawer to cube, then to case. All of your clothes are visible this way, rather than piled on top of each other, so you can easily find items with ease.

Packing cubes also make unpacking simpler and quicker, and if you have that moment at the airport or en route where you need to put something away or get something out, then this will be a much smoother process and not add stress to your journey. On a shorter trip, packing cubes will allow you to successfully live out of your suitcase if you don't want to or can't fully unpack. On longer trips, you could even take the cubes out intact and pop them straight into the drawers or onto shelves at your final destination.

TIPS FOR TRAVELLING WITH CHILDREN – FOLDING LADY STYLE!

1.

Firstly, give them their own backpack and let them pack it themselves, if they are able to – this gives them responsibility and ownership for their belongings, which, in turn, will make them feel empowered. They will also get great enjoyment and learn a lot in the process. The communication that takes place during the packing stage helps ensure they have what they want on the trip, and when they open their backpack on your travel or at their destination they know what to expect inside it. Children don't always like surprises; they are much better with a plan they know about in advance. Give them some boundaries and ideas on what to pack so they don't pack their whole room (or forget the iPad), but also let them choose what they want to take. You'll be surprised at how much they can enjoy the packing experience, and how it helps them to take charge of unpacking later.

2.

Let go of rules for electronics – the world makes parents feel bad about electronics right now but I for one love them, especially for travel. Make sure you have downloaded some suitable apps and movies in advance. Again, ask your child what they want to watch on the journey. Make sure everything is fully charged and you pack the chargers in an accessible place – your handbag or front section of your hand luggage. If there is a plug available on your journey, take advantage and plug the electronics in. You can buy portable chargers that are perfect for travel and will give you an extra charge if necessary.

3.

Snacks – not all journeys require snacks but I always have some dry snacks in my handbag just in case. Biscuits, crisps or dried fruit can help smooth a moment of tension or tiredness and aren't going to leak or require cleaning a child up.

4.

Travel money – my mum and dad always used to give us (and now they give the kids) £10 as 'airport money'. On reflection, the After Value of this £10 was incredible. Instead of sitting around bored I would go to WH Smith and slowly choose a magazine or book. Then I always had money left for some chocolate or something completely useless. But even the useless thing I bought prevented me from getting bored whilst we waited for our flight. And you can apply this to any type of journey. If it's a car journey, take the kids to the shops before and let them pick out a magazine and something else for their backpacks. Even as an adult I allow myself to buy a treat at the airport. It's a great way to take up some time and get in the holiday spirit/diffuse racing-to-the-airport stress.

5.

Stay calm and breathe – travelling can often get stressful, but your mindset will help you keep the pressure under control. Travelling with kids is hard work but remembering that the travel is usually the shortest part of the holiday makes it easier to get through it. Go with the conviction that you will keep your cool, and accept that the situation is out of routine so there may be some hiccups in behaviour. Set the right expectations and I guarantee you will handle it better.

USEFUL TRAVEL FOLDS

COAT PACK

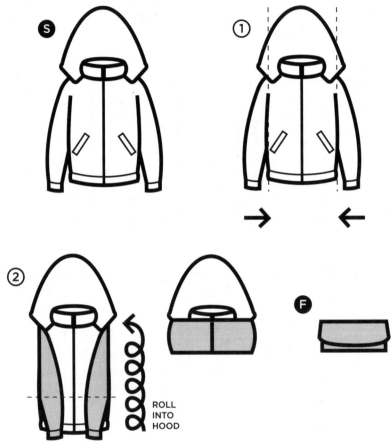

S

① → ←

② ROLL INTO HOOD

F

Coats are so bulky but we have an unexplainable need to always take a coat just in case the weather gets cold or it rains. This next fold will show you how to fold a coat so it stays compact and as small as possible. This fold also works with hoodies and you can add clothes to it if you want to keep everything together.

BEACH TOWEL PACK

When you get to the end of your day at the beach or by the pool the last thing you want to do is put all the wet items in the bag with the dry ones. This super-useful fold will show you how to keep everything together in a towel so you can separate them out later. I always use this after I've been swimming at the gym.

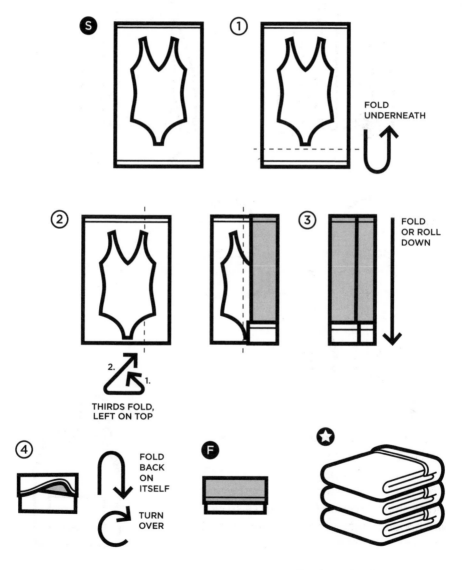

THE OUTFIT PACK

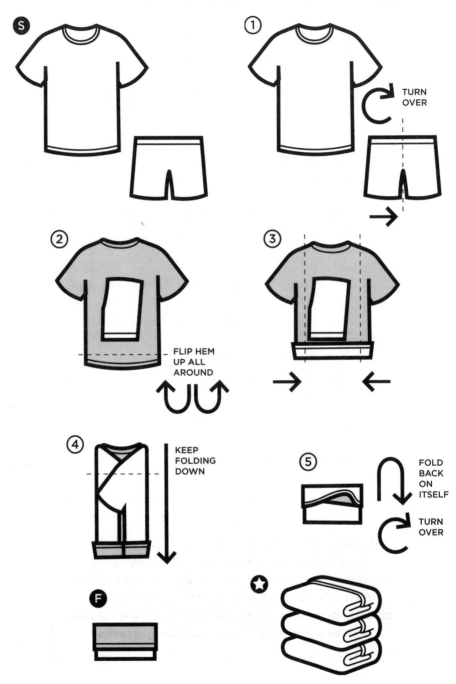

S

1 TURN OVER

2 FLIP HEM UP ALL AROUND

3

4 KEEP FOLDING DOWN

5 FOLD BACK ON ITSELF / TURN OVER

F

IMPORTANT POINTS ABOUT TRAVEL

► If you are a frequent traveller, invest in a good-quality suitcase and passport holder.

► Use the front pocket of your hand luggage for things that may just make your travelling that little bit easier.

► Unpack as soon as you arrive at your destination to get settled and avoid clothes creases – packing cubes make this easy.

► Keep calm when travelling with children and remember that the travelling is the shortest part of the holiday.

My favourite travel products are:

• A quality suitcase – if you are a frequent traveller, then this will be an investment that will bring huge After Value
• Packing cubes – one set per traveller
• Backpacks – any travel storage that is also hands-free is a winner for me!

My favourite travel fold is:

• The outfit pack

TIP
Sometimes it's useful to take some spare clothes.
You might be planning a swim, need spares for
the kids, or expecting to get wet. Whatever the reason,
the outfit pack is a nice way to fold a number of
clothing items into one neat package that will not take
up lots of room and keeps everything together.

GIFT
WRAPPING

Gift wrapping is massively popular on my Instagram and TikTok pages, and what I think people love about it is how satisfying it is. Some people think that just because the paper gets ripped off in seconds it's not key to the gift experience, but that's not the part that brings the After Value. The After Value is for the wrapper as a way to add extra care and love to the 'gift of giving' (and some will find it a calming and mindful activity). For the recipient looking at the effort that was put into the wrap, and for everyone who sees such a pleasing result, this is an extra offering and gesture of respect for the giftee.

When I gift wrapped something in the store, I used to think about the moment the recipient would open it. Even that bit of tissue paper makes the purchase more special, and not all wraps are extravagant or complicated. Gift wrapping gives me the same feeling as I get when folding clothes. Enjoy the choosing of the paper and maybe the ribbon or extras – pick your recipient's favourite colours or choose something that matches the occasion.

Paper choice is personal preference – often the more expensive the paper, the thicker it is. (If you want to use double-sided sticky tape, I recommend a thinner paper as it is usually strong enough to hold the paper in place.) Tissue paper is also making a comeback, and there are wonderful coloured and patterned papers available now. Because of working in the store, I love working with tissue paper as you can use it to wrap many types of gifts without using sticky tape. This was our go-to wrap for customers' purchases and I include it on page 210. We didn't have time for tape (nor could we ever find any) so this wrap is perfect for last-minute wrapping moments. And last year I discovered plant-based sticky tape which I rate highly as it rips easily with no need for scissors. You might go out for a walk just to pick a flower or some foliage to decorate your wrap. All this effort will get you excited to start wrapping, and I also find that when you put more effort into the wrap, you're less likely to leave it until the last minute!

The gift-wrapping resources I always have in stock are:

- **Gift wrap organiser** – this is a box I bought online that has space for everything from rolls of wrap to compartments for ribbons, etc. I find it really useful to keep everything organised, and it also acts as a boundary otherwise my house would be filled with beautiful wrapping paper and ribbons!

- **Tape** – wow... There are a lot of different types of tape! My favourite might just be the clear tape that peels off again simply if you've made a mistake. It's so easy!

- **Tape dispenser** – this makes the whole process so much quicker as you don't faff around needing three hands to cut the tape.

- **Wired ribbon** – wired ribbon is easier to work with if you are not so handy at tying a bow like me. It holds the shape of the bow and is simple to adjust at the end.

- **Small cards** – if you want to add a small message to your gift but a big card is too much, have some small blank token cards to hand.

- **Gift labels** – gifts like wine bottles don't really have a space for cards so a label works better. Labels are also handy if you forget the card!

- **Good scissors** – these are so important and good scissors do not have to be expensive. Keep these in your gift-wrapping organiser.

The wraps I've chosen below are the ones that went viral on TikTok and Instagram last year and are the proven favourites of my followers.

DIAGONAL WRAP

This is a simple hack that may not work every time but is worth a try if you are in that situation we've all found ourselves in where we haven't cut enough wrapping paper and we're just that touch too short...

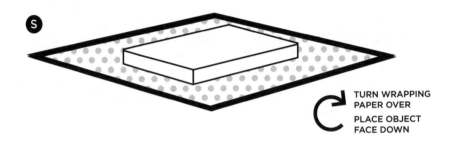

S

TURN WRAPPING
PAPER OVER

PLACE OBJECT
FACE DOWN

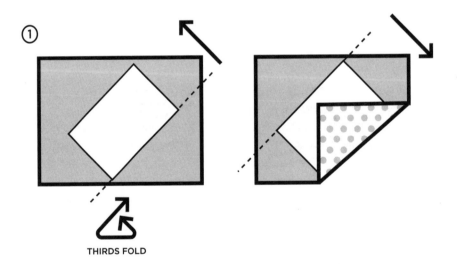

①

THIRDS FOLD

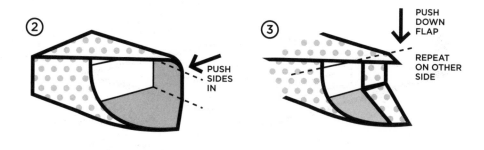

② PUSH SIDES IN

③ PUSH DOWN FLAP
REPEAT ON OTHER SIDE

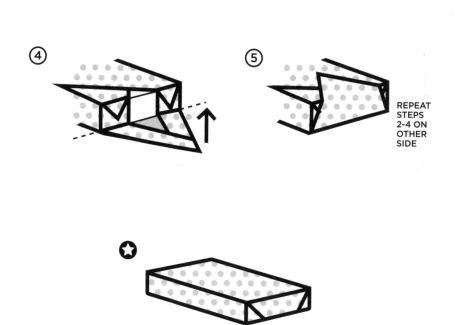

④

⑤ REPEAT STEPS 2-4 ON OTHER SIDE

★

CREATING A PRESENT POUCH WRAP

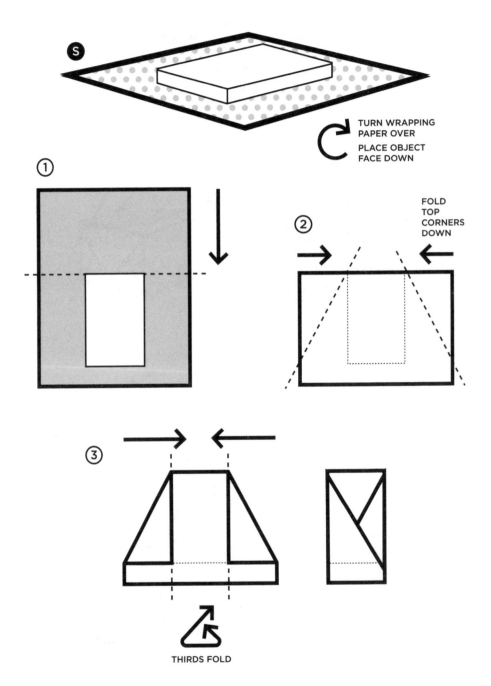

S

TURN WRAPPING PAPER OVER

PLACE OBJECT FACE DOWN

①

② FOLD TOP CORNERS DOWN

③ THIRDS FOLD

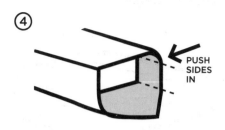

4 → PUSH SIDES IN

5 THIRDS FOLD

F

★

This one is a fun wrap for rectangular items. I love that it creates a pouch that you can pop the card into along with a small gift, some sweets or flowers maybe.

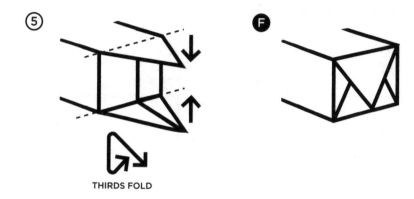

WRAPPING WITH TISSUE PAPER/NO TAPE WRAP

I learnt this next wrap from working in the shop – it's simple and game-changing! We would wrap customer purchases this way before we put them in the bag and what's great about this is that you don't need any tape or stickers, just the tissue paper. It works well for wrapping clothes and boxed/square items, and once practised turns into a rather addictive quick and easy go-to wrap. I use this so much and always have tissue paper handy at home.

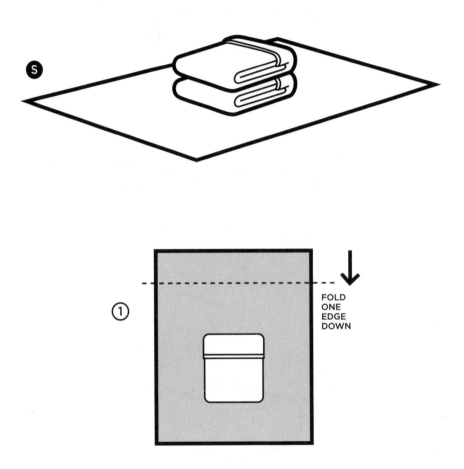

FOLD
ONE
EDGE
DOWN

②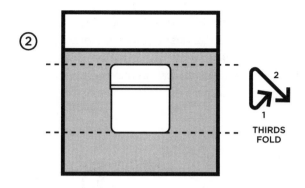

THIRDS
FOLD

③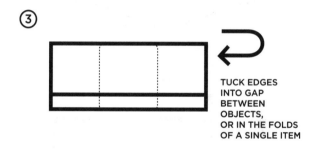

TUCK EDGES
INTO GAP
BETWEEN
OBJECTS,
OR IN THE FOLDS
OF A SINGLE ITEM

GIFT-BAG WRAP

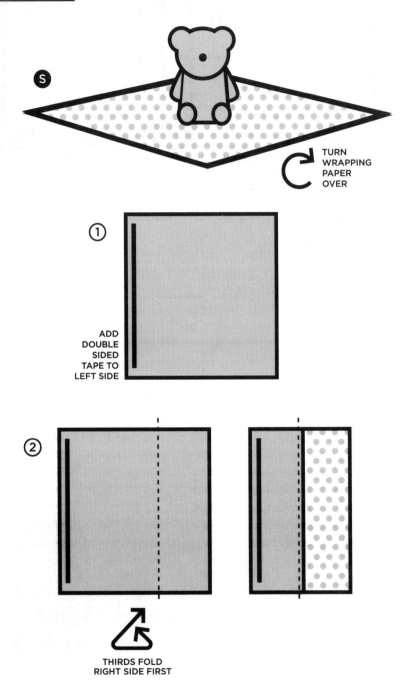

S

TURN WRAPPING PAPER OVER

① ADD DOUBLE SIDED TAPE TO LEFT SIDE

② THIRDS FOLD RIGHT SIDE FIRST

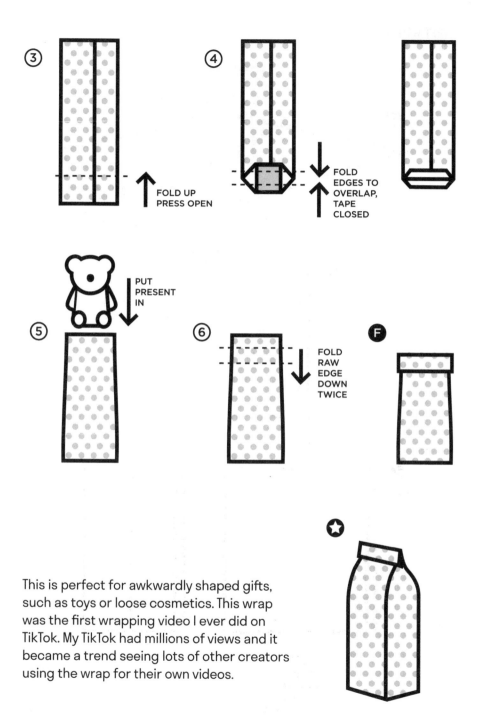

③ FOLD UP PRESS OPEN

④ FOLD EDGES TO OVERLAP, TAPE CLOSED

⑤ PUT PRESENT IN

⑥ FOLD RAW EDGE DOWN TWICE

F

★

This is perfect for awkwardly shaped gifts, such as toys or loose cosmetics. This wrap was the first wrapping video I ever did on TikTok. My TikTok had millions of views and it became a trend seeing lots of other creators using the wrap for their own videos.

CYLINDER WRAP

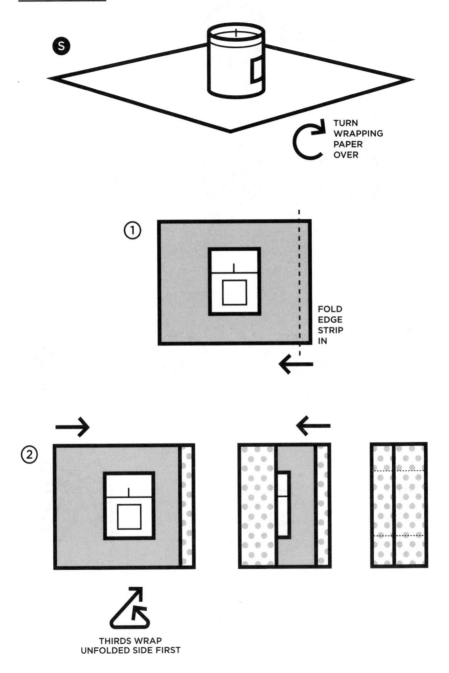

S

TURN
WRAPPING
PAPER
OVER

① FOLD
EDGE
STRIP
IN

② THIRDS WRAP
UNFOLDED SIDE FIRST

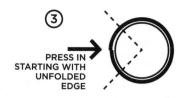

③ PRESS IN
STARTING WITH
UNFOLDED
EDGE

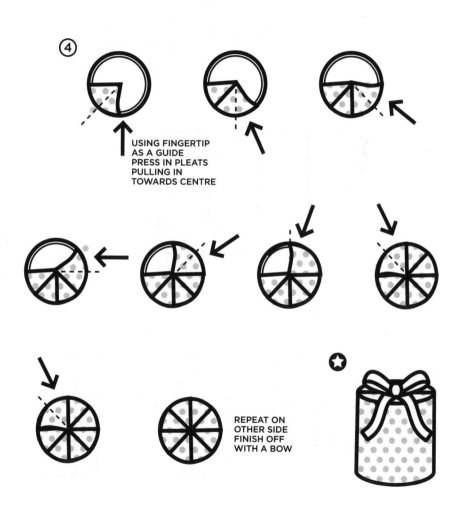

④ USING FINGERTIP
AS A GUIDE
PRESS IN PLEATS
PULLING IN
TOWARDS CENTRE

REPEAT ON
OTHER SIDE
FINISH OFF
WITH A BOW

FUROSHIKI WRAP AND MAKING A BOW

The furoshiki wrap is a new way to wrap for me. It is a centuries-old tradition from Japan – a way to transport and wrap presents and stock. You wrap using a piece of fabric which can be an official wrapping fabric you buy or you can re-purpose something like a scarf. You can also make a bow and add that to any gift, for a bit of extra fun!

I hope that these folding ideas make gifting more fun for you. We've all been there – racing to get to an event and trying to find the end of the sticky tape and a piece of wrapping paper or gift bag of the right size. This way of presenting your gifts to loved ones takes up no extra time once you have practised a few times, and will give such After Value to you and them. When you choose a gift for someone special, simple ways to add that extra pizzazz will make you feel all good inside.

IMPORTANT POINTS FOR GIFT WRAPPING:

► All good wrapping experiences start with having everything to hand, especially if you have a lot of wrapping to do (that's when it's helpful to have a pair of strong scissors within reach).

► A ribbon or bow makes any gift look special, even if wrapped in haste. Mis-matching the ribbon or bow with the wrapping paper is also is an easy way to make something look special and upmarket.

► Children's toys or things that require 'setting up' after opening can sometimes be better presented with a huge bow or ribbon rather than wrapped in the box.

► Enjoy the wrapping experience – it's great to get creative. And if you're not in the mood, then wrapping in front of a good film with snacks to hand makes it easier.

My favourite gift-wrapping products are:

- Clear peelable sticky tape
- Strong scissors
- Patterned tissue paper

My favourite gift-wrapping folds are:

- All of them – gift wrapping is fun!

FINAL THOUGHTS

Everything must come from within. An emotional connection to your living space makes for a sustainable system of organisation plus a way of living that makes your day easier, calmer and brighter. And if that emotional connection is simply that you love looking at your bathroom or your make-up table, that's okay. Folding can be about display and accessible living, as well as part of a big RESET or healthy purge. Make those open spaces motivating and inspiring and let the good vibes flood into your home. I want you to use your home to attract the life you dream of living.

And remember – we're not looking for a fix for 'mess'. We love mess – mess is the sign of a good time, of a life lived. We've just made mess quicker to tidy up and found a way to make life easier and to work out what's really important to you. Folding and After Value bring focus to your surroundings, and help you find peace with the space you have. No rules, no judgement – you can do this!

***

So that's it – you made it to the end! I really hope you are excited to use some of my folds, my organisation hints and tips and my thoughts about After Value and RESETs in your home. If you haven't already, visit my TikTok and Instagram pages for more ideas and thoughts.

Let me know how you get on! Love Sophie x

#foldingfam #thefoldinglady

Website – thefoldinglady.com

Instagram – /thefoldinglady

TikTok – /TheFoldingLady

Pinterest – /TheFoldingLady

YouTube – /TheFoldingLady

Facebook – /TheFoldingLady

WHAT I
LOOK AT AND
LISTEN TO

INSTAGRAM AND TIKTOK FAVES

@Aelishandersonacupuncture –
Five Elements Acupuncture
@Bp3underwear – body positivity
@beckirabin – mindset
@clean_with_jen – cleaning
@carolinehirons – skincare
@courtneycoxofficial – no
explanation needed
@darylandenner – family life/
fashion
@deepakchopra – meditation
@galeyalix – home décor/positivity
@gocleanco – cleaning
@jacobliard – husband
@just_chill_mama – sleep
consultant
@majimb.o – comedian
@megan_rose_lane – body
positivity/spirituality
@nancy.birtwhistle – baking and
eco friendly living
@navy_tux_home – events
@organizewithtracy – professional
US-based organiser
@russellbrand – spiritual/
educational
@stable.fit – fitness
@steven – business and self help
@superprimesurrey – property
@thebirdspapaya – body positivity
@thebodycoach – health and
fitness

@thecompletioncoach – life coach
and crystals
@thesuffolknest – floristry
@trinnywoodall – make-up/
skincare/body positive fashion

Accounts I love on TikTok:
@itscaitlinhello – comedy
@itsdanielmac – interviewer of the
public
@jkentrn – home/asmr
@kyronhamilton – comedy
@lukemillingtondrake – comedy
@monicageldart – comedy
@sulheejessica – making lunch for
her kids!
@texasbeeworks – bee keeper
@thep00lguy – pool maintainence
@theyeeetbaby – general
cuteness
@twojays2 – dancing
@willsmith
@yoleendadong – comedian
@zachking – magic

PODCASTS I LOVE TO LISTEN TO

Deepak Chopra's Infinite Potential
Fat Mascara (beauty podcast hosted by Jessica Matlin and Jennifer
  Goldstein)
Fearne Cotton's Happy Place
Paul McKenna's Positivity Podcast
The Chris Moyles Show on Radio X Podcast (my go to)
The Diary of a CEO with Steven Bartlett

MY TOP 7 TIKTOK FOLDS

Here are my most viewed TikToks, and I promise these are a lot of fun!

Ranger Roll Towel
Views: 35.3 million | Likes: 3.8 million | Shares: 303.9k
Viral in these countries: US, UK, Canada, Australia,
Philippines, Netherlands
Sound used: New Rules (Acoustic) – Dua Lipa

Ranger Fold Towel
Views: 31.5 million | Likes: 2.9 million | Shares: 129.1k
Viral in these countries: US, Philippines, UK, Australia,
Canada, South Africa

Diagonal Wrapping Hack
Views: 13 million | Likes: 1.4 million | Shares: 10.9k
Viral in these countries: US, Indonesia, Thailand,
Philippines, Mexico, UK
Sound used: ASMR of the sound of the wrapping
paper

Folding Calvin Klein Boxers
Views: 8.1 million | Likes: 494.6k | Shares: 31k
Viral in these countries: UK, Germany, France,
Netherlands, Australia, Mexico
Sound used: Rock Around The Clock – Bill Haley & His
Comets

Organising Your Sock Drawer
Views: 8.7 million | Likes: 1.2 million | Shares: 23.7k
Viral in these countries: US, UK, Denmark, Canada, Poland, Australia
Sound used: Celebrate the Good Times – Mason

Folding Toddler Tights
Views: 5.2 million | Likes: 322k | Shares: 7,021
Viral in these countries: US, UK, Germany, France, Italy, Poland
Sound used: Coming of Age – Blondes

Sock Ranger Roll
Views: 4.8 million | Likes: 462k | Shares: 5.4k
Viral in these countries: US, UK, Canada, Philippines, South Africa, Australia
Sound used: Famous (I'm the One) – Mozzy & Iamsu!

Thank you for all your support along the way x

GLOSSARY OF
TRANSLATIONS

Having followers all around the world means a lot of translations. We have such fun with this online so I had to give it a section in the book... enjoy!

What I say...	What you say...
Airing cupboard	Hot press/linen closet
Baby grow	Onesie
Bedside table	Nightstand
Biscuits	Cookies
Brew	Cup of tea
Buzzin'	Pleased
Chest of drawers	Dresser
Chuffed	Happy
Creases	Wrinkles
Crisps	Chips
Cupboard	Cabinet
Dungarees	Overalls
Duvet	Doona
Flannel	Face cloth, wash cloth
Flat/maisonette	Apartment
Flip flop	Thong
Holiday	Vacation
I have a washing machine in my kitchen	That's weird
Joggers	Sweatpants
Jumper	Sweater
Knickers	Panties, underwear
Loo	Washroom
Nappy	Diaper
Pram/buggy	Stroller
Pudding	Dessert
Rubbish	Trash
Sausage roll	What's that?
Secondary school	High school
Sweets	Candy
Tea	Dinner
Trainers	Sneakers
Trousers	Pants
Wellies	Rainboots

THANKS

Firstly, it goes without saying that my biggest thank you goes to the #foldingfam. There would be no reason for this book without you, and I am forever grateful for every single one of you. The time you take to send me messages and watch my content blows my mind; every share, every comment and every save means so much because it makes the family grow and keeps it alive. I wrote this book for you all! Massive thank you to my book agent, Kim Whalen, for navigating me through my first book from beginning to end. I would write another book just to keep our chats going! Louise Bay, I am so grateful you introduced us. And to Sarah Hornsley – thank you for getting us off to a great start.

Thank you to Lauren and Liv and the team at Yellow Kite for believing that me writing a book could even be a thing. And then to Marta and the team at HarperCollins for believing it could be a thing in the US and Canada. This has been a dream opportunity that I am so grateful for.

James Ward, thank you for bringing The Folding Lady alive, for translating my vision into the book, and for listening to my rambling voice notes in the process. Thank you to Lydia Blagden for bringing all the folds to life and putting up with me through that process!

To Miss Rhiannon Tims, there would have been no folding had it not been for our TikTok games in lockdown. You started something amazing with me and I will always love you for that.

To my family and friends – Mum, Dad, Philippa, Alban, Kel, Dean, Teddy, Beau, Ellie, Elliot, Gran, John, Cheryl, Jordan, Mark, Macy, Aelish, Vhairi – thank you for supporting me day to day, keeping things normal, and for checking in and being excited!

To my George, as a teenager you've had mixed emotions about your mum becoming TikTok famous, and rightly so! When the pre-orders were announced and you shared my post on your story for the first time acknowledging I was in fact your mum, it was something special. Thank you for the support in your teenage ways. I love you so much.

Arthur, you have no idea what is going on even though you've been one of the people who has been with me the most while I did all of the writing and deserve your spot in the acknowledgements. Thanks for waking up at 6am every day and playing so nicely giving me time to write. I love you so much. I should also thank CBeebies, Netflix, Amazon Prime and Disney+ for contributing to this as well.

TikTok – you started me on a journey that got me to this point, thank you!

And finally to Jacob. . . you are, by far, my most favourite person on the team. I love you x

The Folding Lady behind
the scenes ft. Arthur

NOTES

books to help you live a good life

Join the conversation and tell
us how you live a #goodlife

🐦 @yellowkitebooks
📘 YellowKiteBooks
📌 Yellow Kite Books
📷 YellowKiteBooks